Copyright © 2016 by Helmy Alexcia

All rights reserved, which includes the rights to reproduce portions or entirety of this book.

Printed and bound in the United States of America.

Cover Design: Helmy Alexcia

Editor: Philip L.Bell, Ardianto R. Tandiono and Leah Chen.

ISBN: 978-1-365-55754-5

Version: 10-2016

QUOTE

So many of our dreams at first seem impossible,

then they seem improbable,

and then, when we summon the will,

they soon become inevitable

~ Christopher Reeve ~

DEDICATION

This book is dedicated to the memory of my mom, Yellis Gunadi.

To my beautiful wife Moira Siswoyo, my beautiful daughter, Shannon Joy, my handsome son, Josh Sebastian and all my brothers and sisters in New Zealand and Indonesia.

I hope I make you guys proud.

ABOUT THE AUTHOR

My name is Helmy Alexcia and I am a Developer and Report Writer. When my career in IT began as a Data Analyst Consultant I noticed the lack of resources available to quickly familiarize one-self with developing and writing reports. Between a demanding occupation and maintaining peace in a home with two boisterous toddlers and my lovely wife, I realized that there had to be a more simple way to independently gain this knowledge without constantly turning to my colleagues for guidance. But there was nothing of such sort available on the market during the time. Through the mentorship of my superiors and extensive experience working with various companies, I swiftly advanced to the positions of a Developer and Report Writer. Throughout my career I have gained fluency in numerous Report Designer tools such as Crystal Reports, SSRS, Tableau in SQL, and Oracle Environment.

This book is meant to serve as the straightforward crash course that I never had to guide you through efficiently designing and developing reports. Upon completion you will have a comprehensive knowledge of the methods and strategies behind the job in order to confidently "jumpstart" your career as a Report Writer.

ACKNOWLEDGMENTS

I would extend my gratitude to my cousin, Christina Bell, for her cheerful encouragement and unwavering support during my journey of writing this book.

Also a special thanks to my editors, Philip L. Bell, Ardianto R. Tandiono, and Leah Chen, for their dedication and insightful feedback.

More thanks to my beautiful wife, Moira Siswoyo, for her beaming love and support and to my daughter, Shannon Joy, who often enthusiastically requests updates on the progress of this book.

Finally, I'd like to express my appreciation to those who purchase this book. I hope you found what you needed and enjoyed it as much as I did writing it!

Thank you for all your support!

CONNECT WITH ME

If you have any questions, ideas, comments, or need the files that I used in this book, please email them to me at:

koel0202@yahoo.com

CONTENTS

Chapter 1 - INTRODUCTION   1
    What Is Crystal Reports?   1
    Why Use Crystal Reports?   3
    Getting Started   4
    Report Sections   5
    Toolbar   13
    Repository Explorer   21
    Workbench   21
    Dependency Checker   22

Chapter 2 – DEVELOPING A REPORT   23
    Create a New Connection   23
    Setup ODBC Connection   34
    Create a New Report   41

Chapter 3 – FORMATTING A REPORT   49
    Formatting Toolbar   49
    Field Formatting   57
    Format Editor   64
    Common Tab   64
    Border Tab   71
    Font Tab   75
    Paragraph Tab   79
    Hyperlink Tab   81
    Select Expert   82

CONTENTS

Section Expert	98
Sections	101
Common tab	104
Color	110
Chapter 4 – GROUPING, SUMMARY AND RUNNING TOTAL	**111**
Grouping Data	111
Insert Group	113
Group Expert	117
Group Sort Expert	122
Understanding of Summary	127
Summary Example	131
Running Total	141
Summary	143
Evaluate	144
Reset	144
Chapter 5 – PARAMETER	**150**
Creating a Parameter Field	151
Activate Parameter	155
Assign Parameter	157
P_Excel Parameter	162

CONTENTS

Chapter 6 – FORMULAS AND FUNCTIONS   173
    What Is Formula?   173
    Create a Simple Formula   173
    Insert and use your Formulas   177
    Operator   179
        1. Arithmetic   180
        2. Arrays   180
        3. Boolean   181
        4. Comparisons   181
        5. Control Structure   181
        6. Other   182
    Sample of formulas   182

Chapter 7 – SUBREPORTS   184
    What Is Subreports?   184
    Type of Subreports   184
    Insert Subreports   185
    Link Subreports   188

Chapter 1 - INTRODUCTION

What Is Crystal Reports?

Crystal Reports is a very powerful report writer design tool that collects data from a variety of data source connections and displays it in easy to read charts, tables, and graphs. The data source connections are **Access/Excel**, **ODBC** (**RDO**) for **SQL**, **OLAP** or **ADO.NET** (**XML**) and many other souce connections, as you can see below in figure 1.0.a, 1.0.b, and 1.0.c.

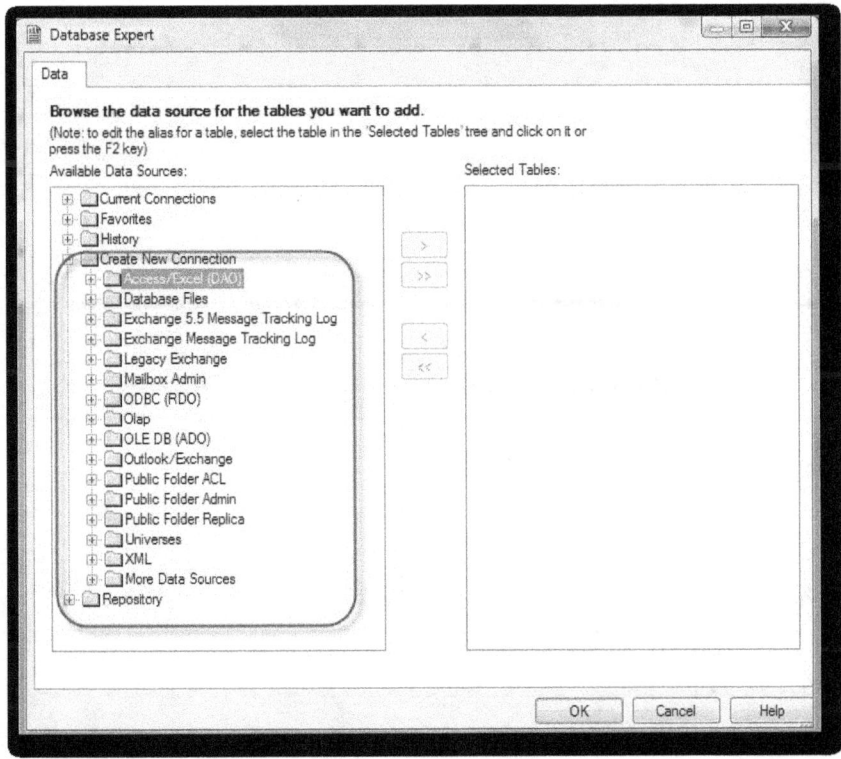

Figure 1.0.a – *Access/Excel* Database connections thru *DAO*

Chapter 1 - INTRODUCTION

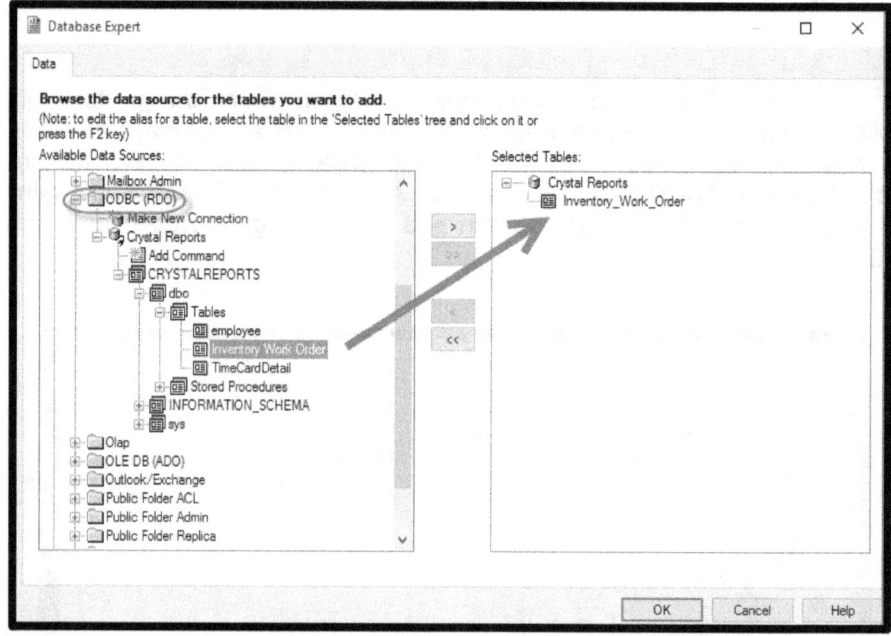

Figure 1.0.b – ODBC Connection to SQL Server

Chapter 1 - INTRODUCTION

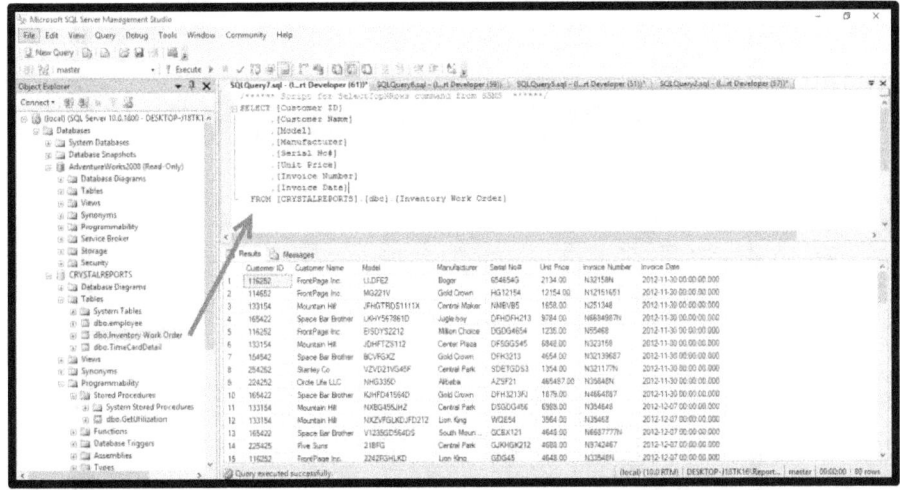

Figure 1.0.c – Inventory Work Order table and their columns in SQL Server

Why Use Crystal Reports?

Crystal Reports combines the power of database programming with the familiar and **EASY-TO-LEARN** Windows application environment. Crystal Reports simplifies the task by allowing users to create **formulas**, **formats**, and templates, which can then be saved and re-used.

Crystal Reports communicates seamlessly with many different output formats including Microsoft **Word**, **Email**, **Excel**, **Adobe PDF**, **Text** and even over the **Web**. Here are the most common formats in Crystal Reports, as shown below in figure 1.1.

Chapter 1 - INTRODUCTION

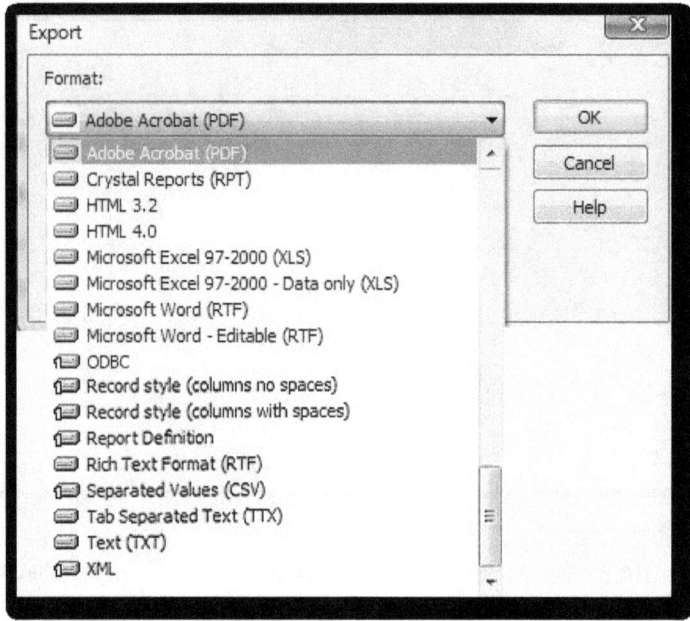

Figure 1.1 – *The* most common formats in Crystal Reports

Getting Started

Now that we've covered a little of what Crystal Reports can do, let's move forward but before we take a look at what you can do with **Crystal Reports**, first, let's look and get to know at **Report Sections,** and the **Design/Preview** Tabs.

Chapter 1 - INTRODUCTION

Report Sections

     Crystal Reports, like Word or Access, uses report sections to arrange and display your data in the manner of your choosing. By default, there are five report sections, but you can add or delete sections as needed. To add one of the sections, simply right click to one of the sections and choose "**Insert Section below**", as shown in below figure 1.2a. The default report sections are: **Report Header**, **Page Header**, **Details**, **Report Footer**, and **Page Footer**. It is important to understand the function and behavior of each Section in order to develop an attractive and presentable report, as shown below in figure *1.2b*.

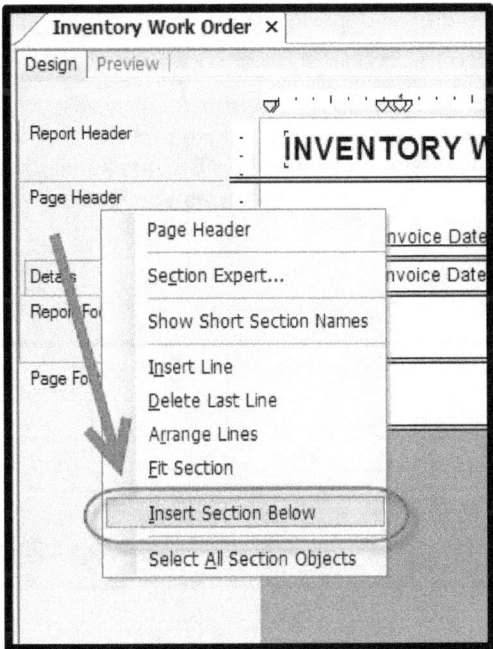

Figure 1.2a – Choose "**Insert Section Below**" to insert a new section

Chapter 1 - INTRODUCTION

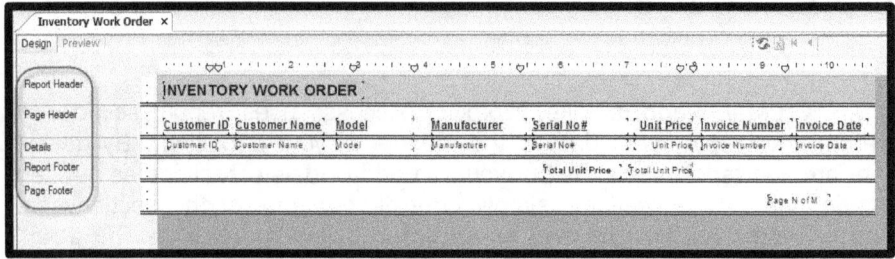

Figure 1.2b – Five basic sections (Design tab)

Report Header

Data and objects in the **Report Header** section will only print on the first page of a report. There is only one Report Header on each report but you can hide or suppress the Report Header by "**Suppress**" it or using of the formulas, which we will cover in later chapters, as shown below in figure *1.3a and 1.3b*.

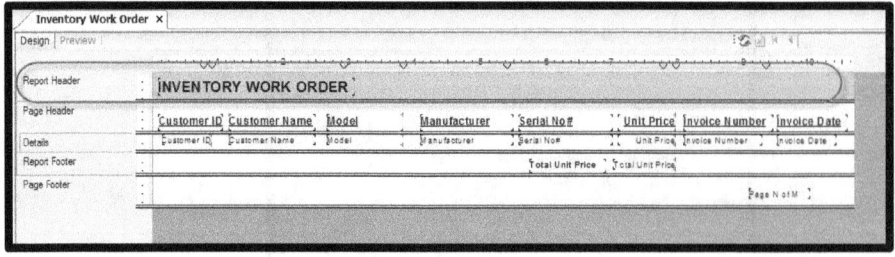

Figure 1.3a – Only one Report Header on each report (Design tab)

Chapter 1 - INTRODUCTION

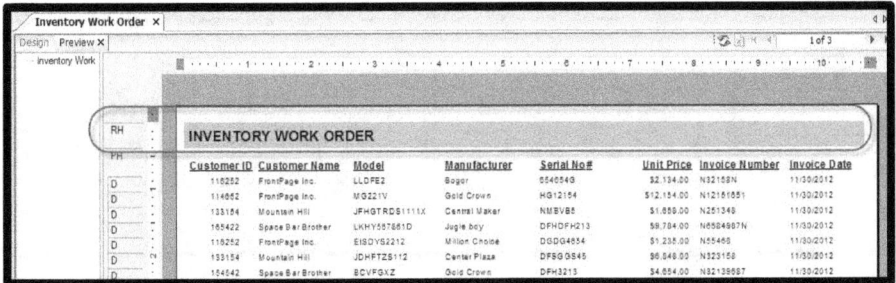

Figure 1.3b – Only one Report Header on each report (Preview tab)

Page Header

Any data and objects in the **Page Header** section print at the top of every page. However, you can customize the Page Header with formulas and/or insert new Page Headers on the report (which will be covered later), as shown below in figure *1.4a and 1.4b*.

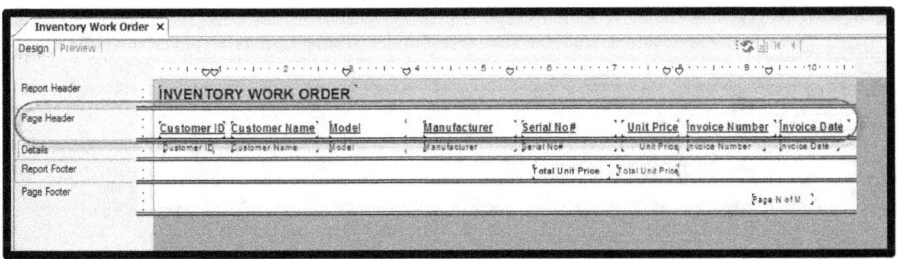

Figure 1.4a – Page Header (Design tab)

Chapter 1 - INTRODUCTION

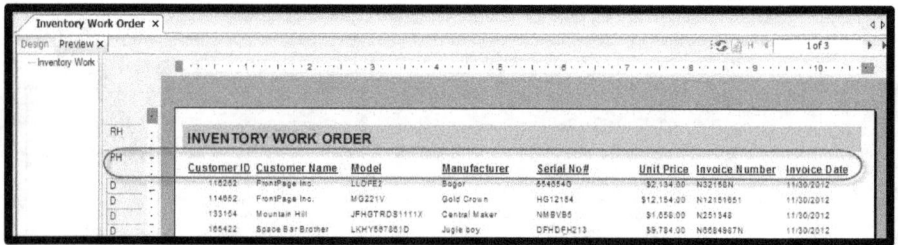

Figure 1.4b – Page Header (Preview tab)

Details

Report data fields are presented in the **Details** section. Each record in the source database will display as a separate line of data in the Details section, so if you have ten records of information in your database, there will be ten lines of "**Details**" in your report. You can customize the Details section with formulas, and insert, hide or change Details according to your needs (Yes, you guessed it! We will cover that in later chapters as well), as shown below in figure *1.5a and 1.5b*.

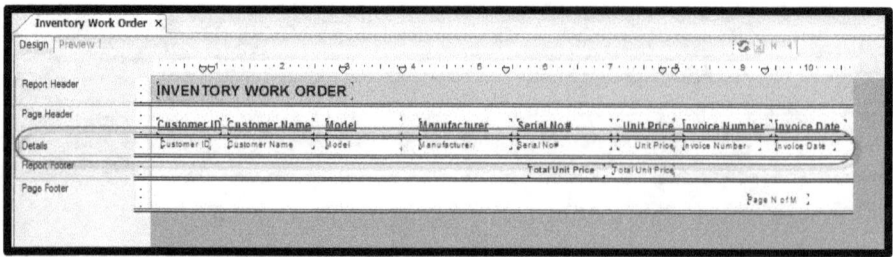

Figure 1.5a – Details (Design tab)

Chapter 1 - INTRODUCTION

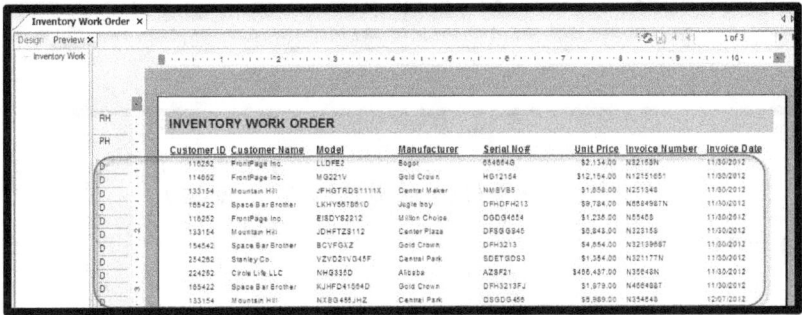

Figure 1.5b – Details (Preview tab)

Report Footer

Summation data such as "**Summary**" and "**Grand Total**" are commonly placed in the *Report Footer* Section. There is only one Report Footer on each report. However, you can customize the Report Footer with a formula and insert a new Report Footer on the report, as shown below in figure *1.6a and 1.6b*.

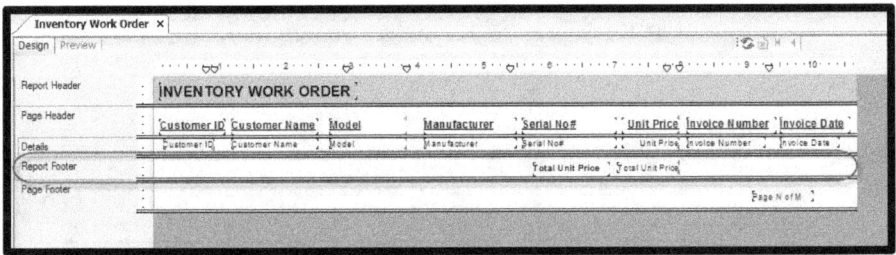

Figure 1.6a – Report Footer (Design tab)

Chapter 1 - INTRODUCTION

Figure 1.6b – Report Footer (Preview tab)

Page Footer

Any data and objects in the **Page Footer** section print at the bottom of every page, but you can hide or suppress the Report Footer with formulas, as shown below in figure *1.7a and 1.7b*.

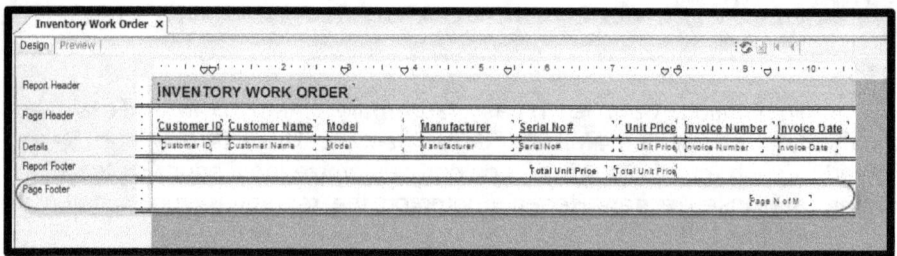

Figure 1.7a – Page Footer (Design tab)

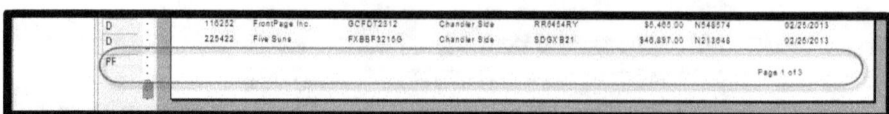

Figure 1.7b – Page Footer (Preview tab)

Chapter 1 - INTRODUCTION

Design Tab

The *Design* tab is the template section where most data is arranged, inserted, and displayed. This is where tasks such as grouping, labeling, calculating, and formatting are done. If you want to import or display an image or a table, you can do that here as well. The Design tab provides an efficient environment for creating a report.

To add data fields to the body of your report, first open the **Field Explorer** tab from the menu bar, select **View**, then click **Field Explorer**. From within the categories of **Database Fields**, **Formula Fields**, **Parameter Fields**, or **Special Fields**, find the name of the item you want to add, and then click, drag, and drop the selected item into your report, as shown below in figure *1.8*.

Chapter 1 - INTRODUCTION

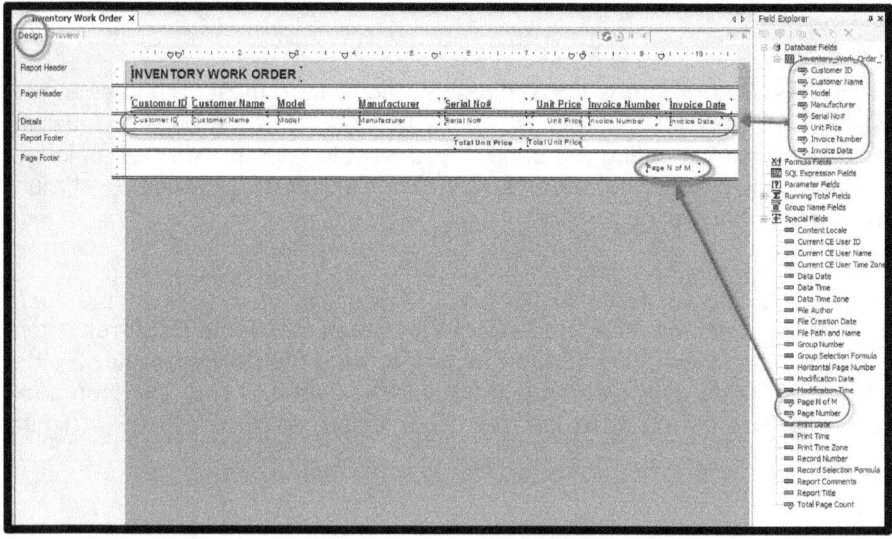

Figure 1.8 – Design tab is the template section where most data is arranged, inserted, and displayed

Preview Tab

The **Preview Tab** allows you to see your document in advance, exactly as it will look when printed. You can use this feature as often as you want while constructing your report to modify, edit, correct, and improve the appearance of your document before printing. The Preview icon looks like a sheet of paper with a magnifying glass in front of it. If it is not visible on the taskbar, click on the **View** tab and click the Preview icon on the drop-down window. It will now stay visible on the taskbar until deselected from the View menu, as shown below in figure *1.9a and 1.9b*.

Chapter 1 - INTRODUCTION

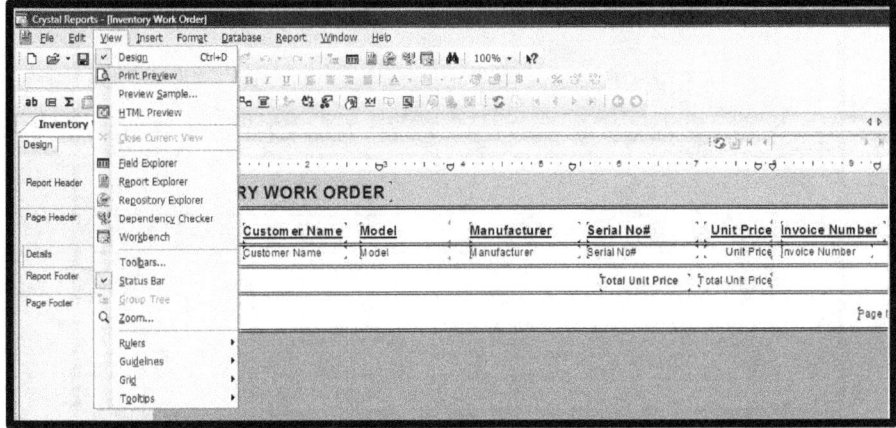

*Figure 1.9a – **Preview tab** allows you to see your document in advance, exactly as it will look when printed*

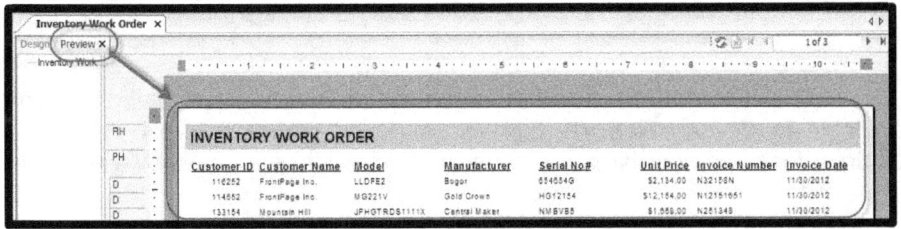

Figure 1.9b – Preview tab

Toolbar

Standard Toolbar

The **Standard Toolbar** lets you create or open an existing report. It is a toolbar which gives you quick access to the main features of **Crystal Reports**, as shown below in figure *1.10*.

Chapter 1 - INTRODUCTION

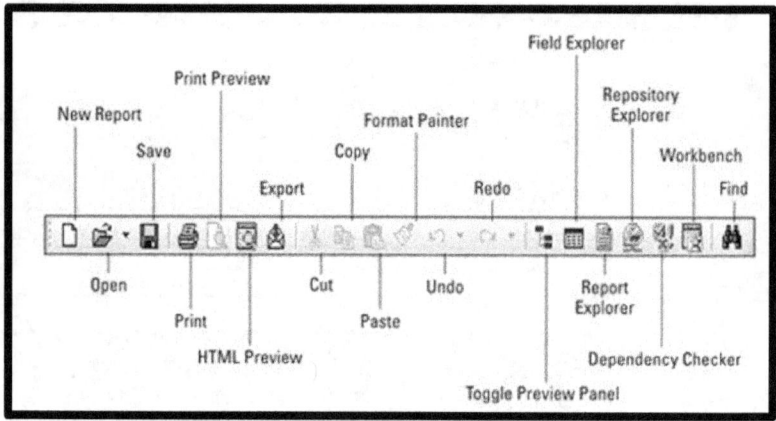

Figure 1.10 – *Standard toolbar*

Formatting Toolbar

The **Formatting Toolbar** displays the various formatting options available to **Crystal Reports** for modifying and setting the text alignment, borders, font size, font type, color, decimal precision, etc., as shown below in figure *1.11*.

Chapter 1 - INTRODUCTION

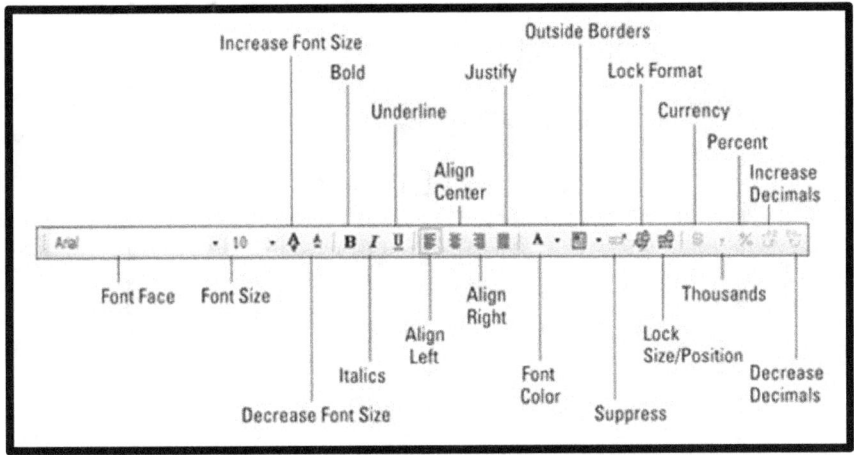

Figure 1.11 – Formatting toolbar

Insert Toolbar

The **Insert Toolbar** allows you to improve the report by adding all kinds of stuff such as images, lines, Summary, and charts, as shown below in figure 1.12.

Chapter 1 - INTRODUCTION

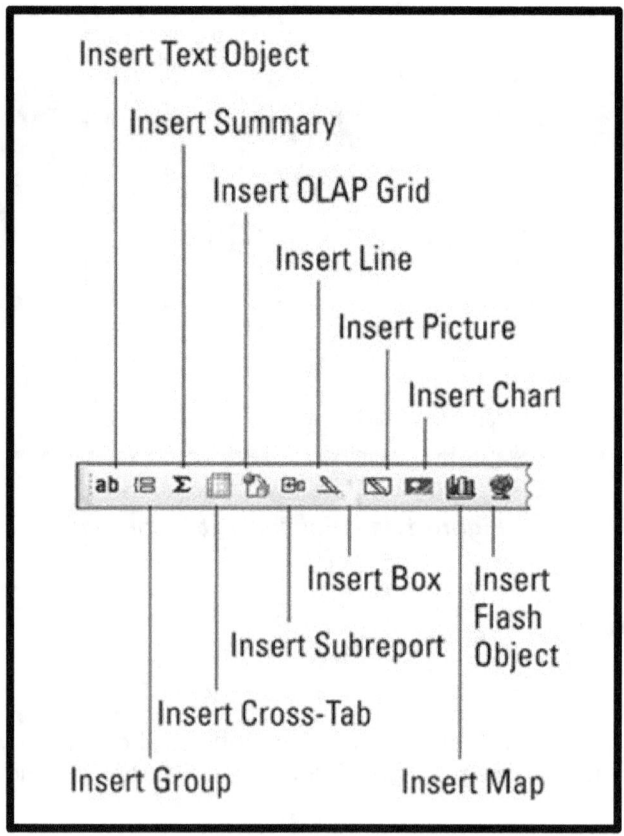

Figure1.12 – Insert toolbar

Expert Toolbar

The **Expert Toolbar** is used to access the **Database**, **Template** and **Group Expert** features, as shown below in figure *1.13*.

Chapter 1 - INTRODUCTION

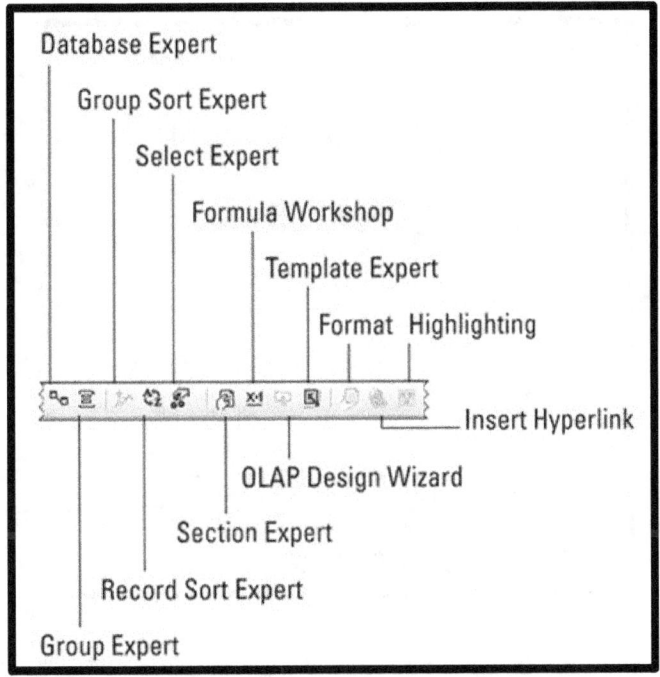

Figure 1.13 – Export toolbar

Navigation Toolbar

The *Navigation Toolbar* allows you to jump quickly to another page, or to the front or back of your report, as shown below in figure *1.14*.

Chapter 1 - INTRODUCTION

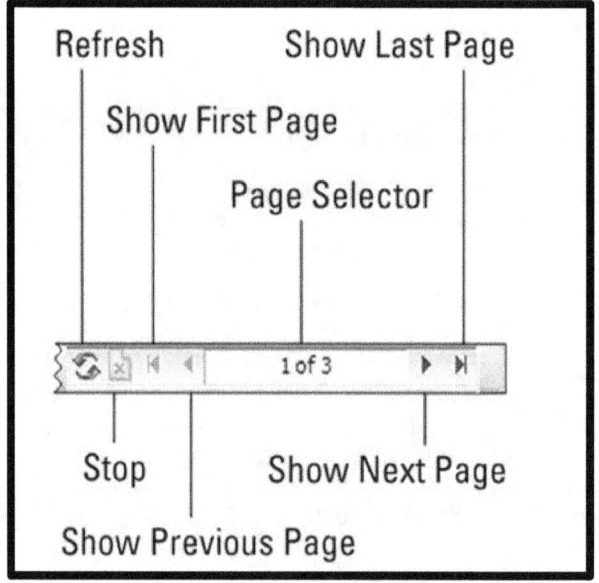

Figure 1.14 – Navigation toolbar

EXPLORER

Field Explorer

The *Field Explorer*, which was mentioned earlier, allows you to insert, modify or delete fields from the body of your report, and/or create **Formulas**, **SQL Expressions**, **Parameters**, **Running Totals**, and other specialized report functions. To activate the Field Explorer, select "**View**" and click "**Field Explorer**", as shown below in figure *1.15*.

Chapter 1 - INTRODUCTION

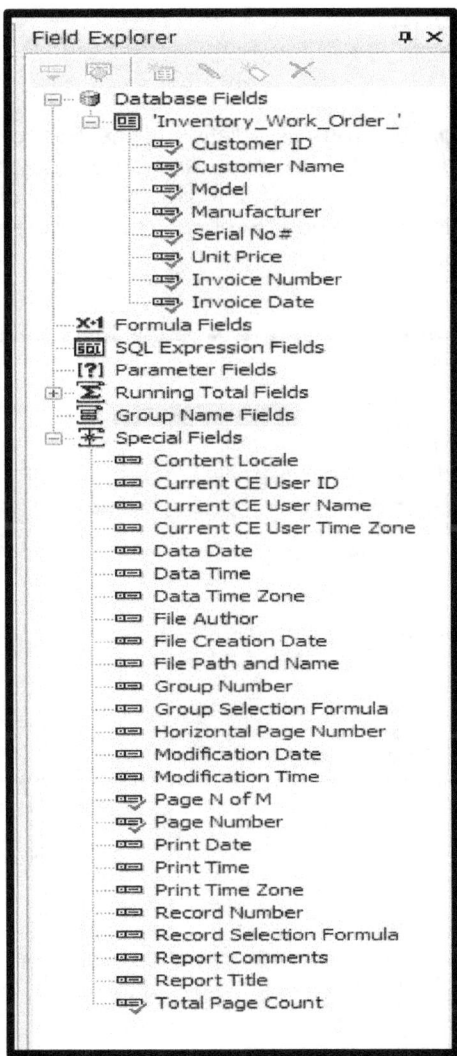

Figure 1.15 – *Field Explorer*

Chapter 1 - INTRODUCTION

Report Explorer

The **Report Explorer** is a listing of the **Section Fields** in the report. The Section Fields are the database and output objects that will appear in your report. You can modify the fields directly by right clicking on the selected field. To activate the Report Explorer, select "**View**" and click "**Report Explorer**", as shown below in figure *1.16*.

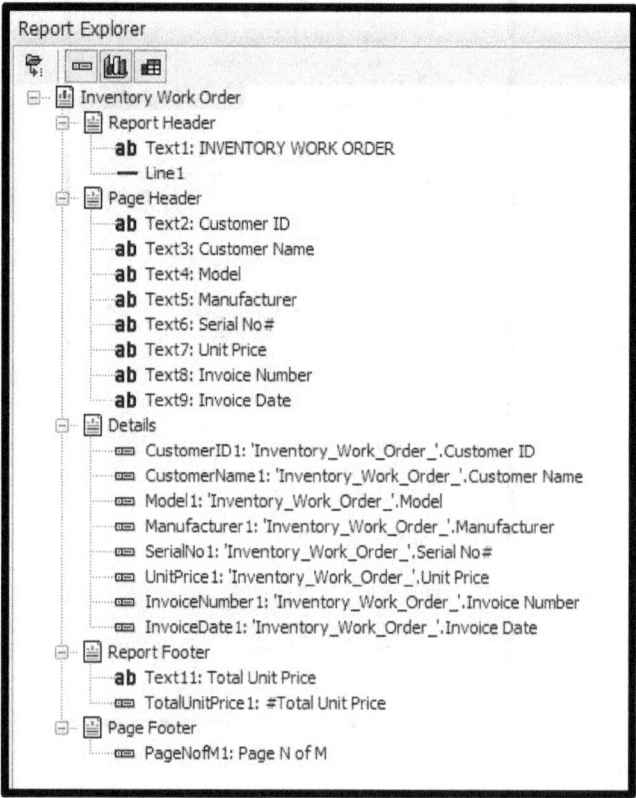

Figure 1.16 – *Report Explorer*

Chapter 1 - INTRODUCTION

Repository Explorer

The **Repository Explorer** allows you to logon to a server with shared access to common objects such as **Text Objects**, **Bitmaps**, and **SQL commands**. In the Repository Explorer, you can create and add reports so other users can access them. To activate the Repository Explorer, just simply select "**View**" and click "**Repository Explorer**", as shown below in figure *1.17*.

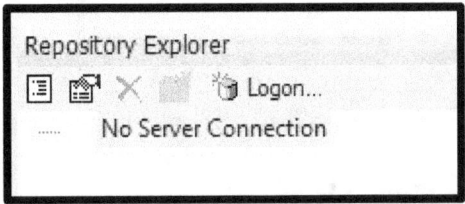

Figure 1.17 – *Repository Explorer*

Workbench

The **Workbench** allows you to create a new folder, rename, move, and reorganize your files to any **File Folders** and **Directories** that you want. To activate Workbench, select "**View**" and click "**Workbench**", as shown below in figure *1.18*.

Chapter 1 - INTRODUCTION

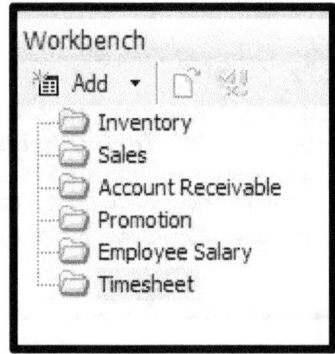

Figure 1.18 – Workbench

Dependency Checker

The **Dependency Checker** is a verification tool that looks for errors in data links, hyperlinks, repository links, formula compilations, etc. To activate the Dependency Checker, select "**View**" and click "**Dependency Checker**", as shown below in figure *1.19*.

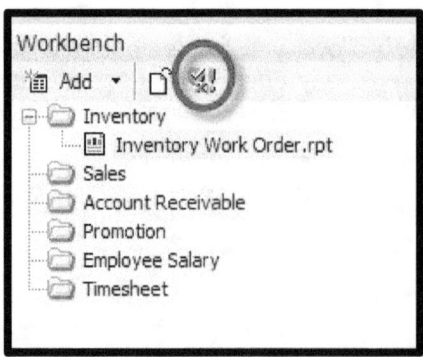

Figure 1.19 – Dependency Checker

Chapter 2 – DEVELOPING A REPORT

Create a New Connection

In this chapter, I am going to show you how to create a new report using the dataset called **Inventory Work Order** from two different data sources connection. One is thru **Access/Excel (DAO)** connection for an excel spreadsheet and second connection is thru **ODBC (RDO)** for Inventory Work Order table in SQL Server. Connecting to a data source is just pointing to a source or location to get the data.

Are you ready? Let's do it! In the **Inventory Work Order** Excel spreadsheet, there are eight columns and eighty-one rows. Each Column has a single header. The headers are: *Customer ID*, *Customer Name*, *Model*, *Manufacturer*, *Serial No*, *Unit Price*, *Invoice Number*, and *Invoice,* as shown below in figure 2.0.

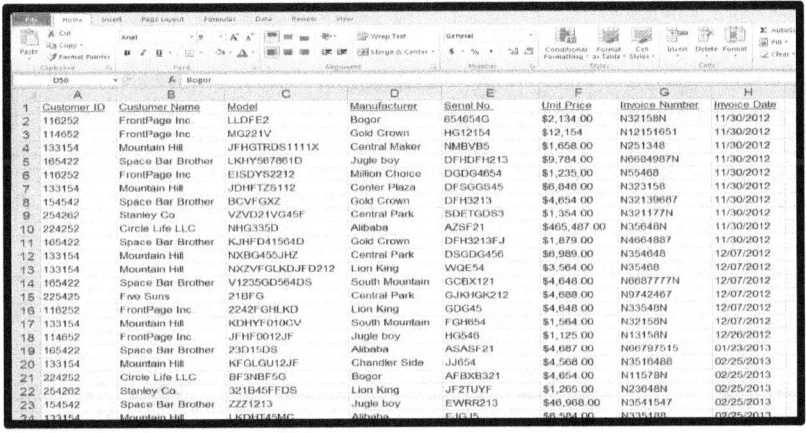

Figure 2.0 – Inventory Work Order spreadsheet

Reporting With Visual Crystal Reports

Chapter 2 – DEVELOPING A REPORT

Let's open **Crystal Reports**. In this book, I am using **Crystal Reports version 11.** Select **File**, **New** and click **Blank Report** or on the start page, click on Blank Report, as shown below in figure 2.1a and 2.1b.

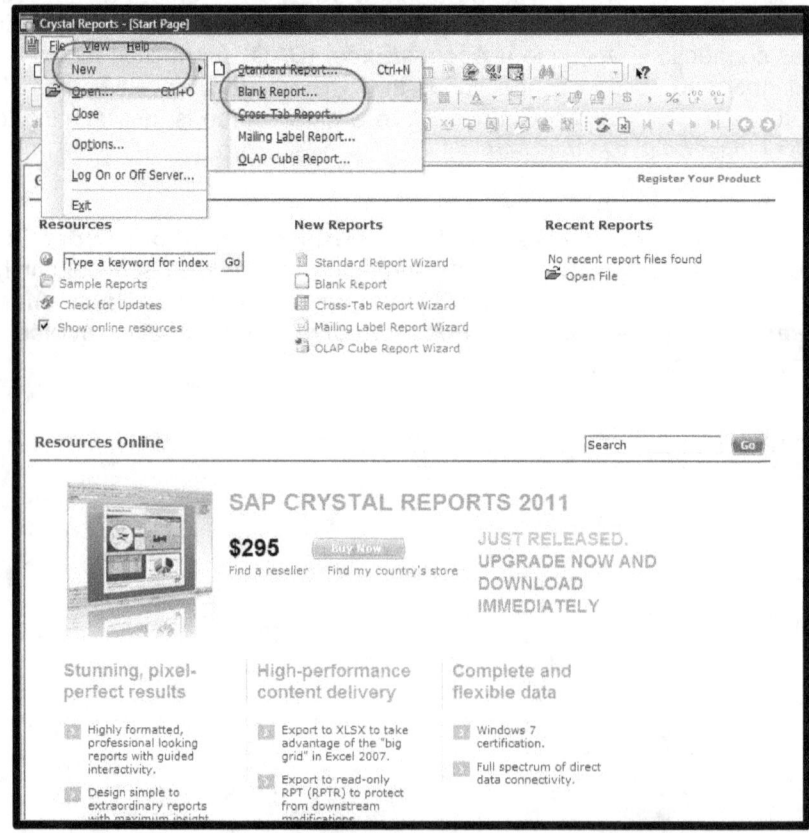

Figure 2.1a – File –> New –> Blank Report

Chapter 2 – DEVELOPING A REPORT

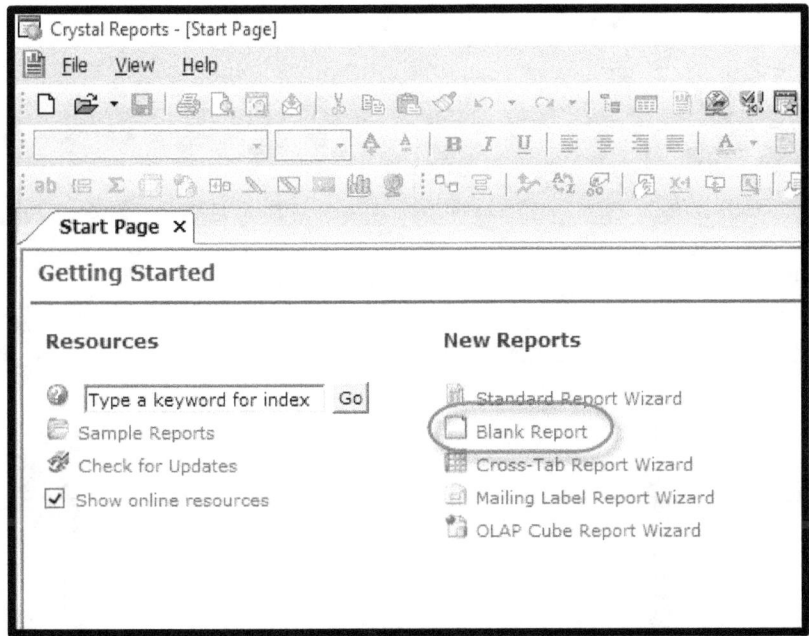

Figure 2.1b – *Blank Report from start page*

Chapter 2 – DEVELOPING A REPORT

Double click **Create New Connection**, as shown below in figure 2.2.

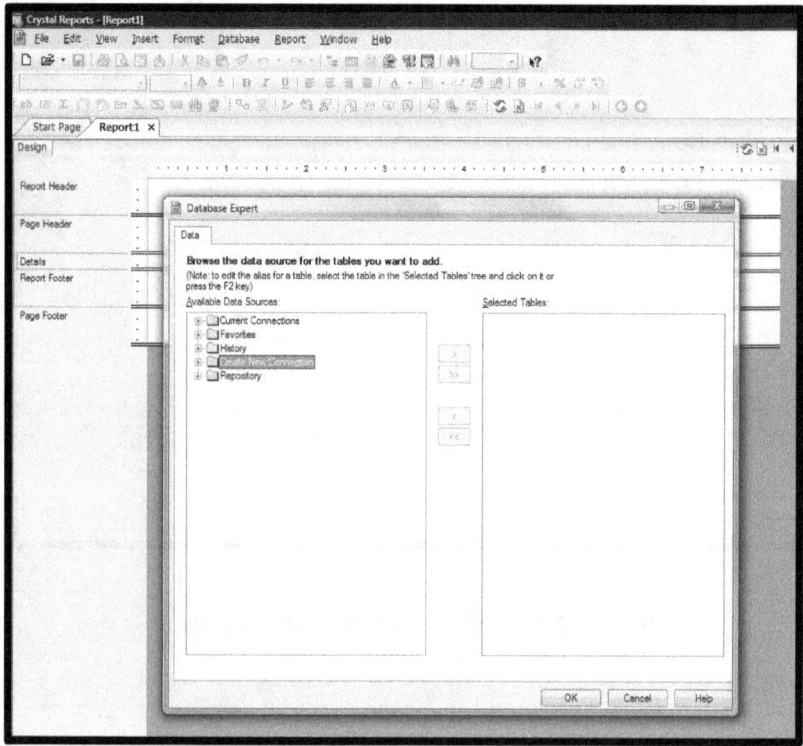

Figure 2.2– Create New Connection

Chapter 2 – DEVELOPING A REPORT

Double click **Access/Excel (DAO)**, as shown below in figure 2.3.

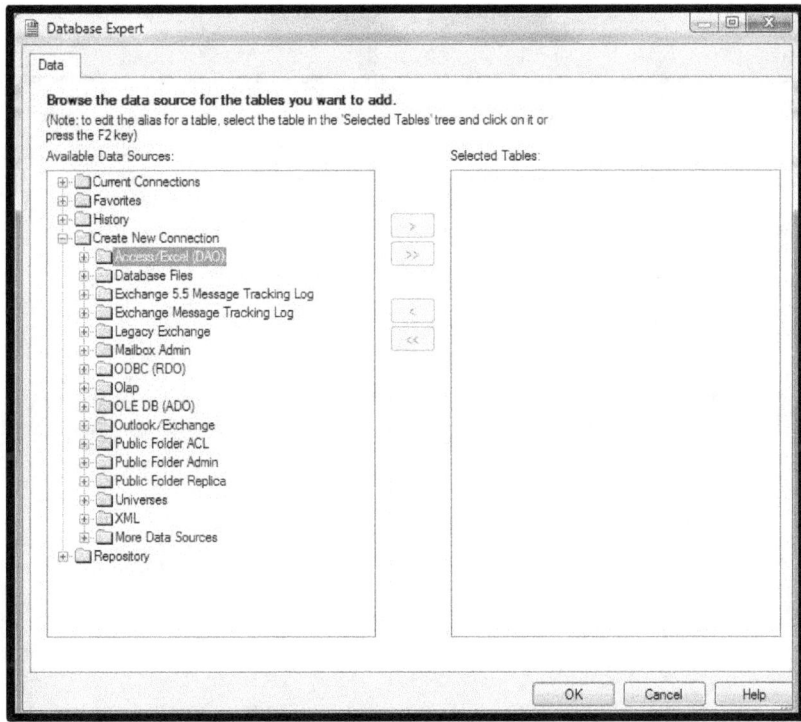

Figure 2.3 – *Access/Excel (DAO)*

Chapter 2 – DEVELOPING A REPORT

Select **Excel 8.0** for the **Database Type,** choose **Inventory Work Order** as a **Database Name**, and then click **Finish**, as shown below in figure 2.4.

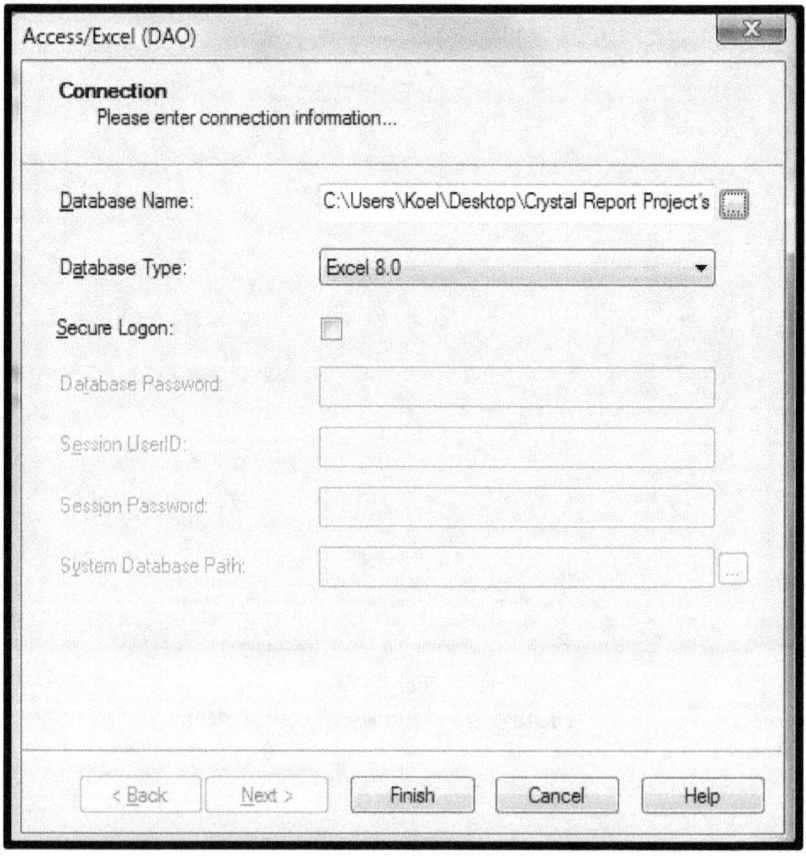

Figure 2.4 – *Database Name and Database Type*

Chapter 2 – DEVELOPING A REPORT

Select **Inventory Work Order** and move it to the **Selected Tables** area by using the right arrow icon **(>)**, then click **OK,** as shown below in figure 2.5.

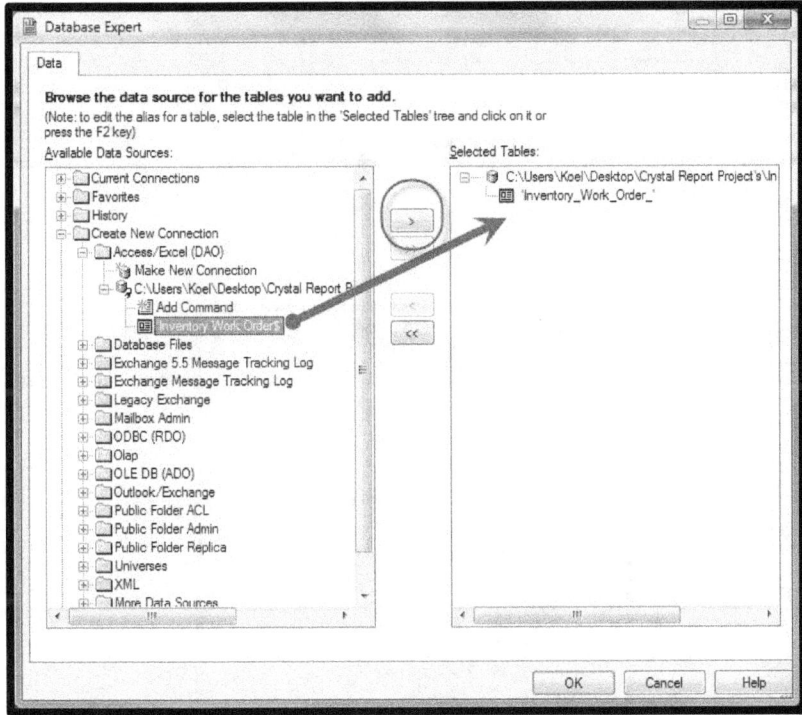

Figure 2.5 – Available Data Source to the Selected Tables

The file "**Inventory_Work_Order_**" appears in the **Database Fields** on the right-hand side. Click the (**+**) sign to expand the **Database Fields** and the selected file, as shown below in figure 2.6a and 2.6b.

Chapter 2 – DEVELOPING A REPORT

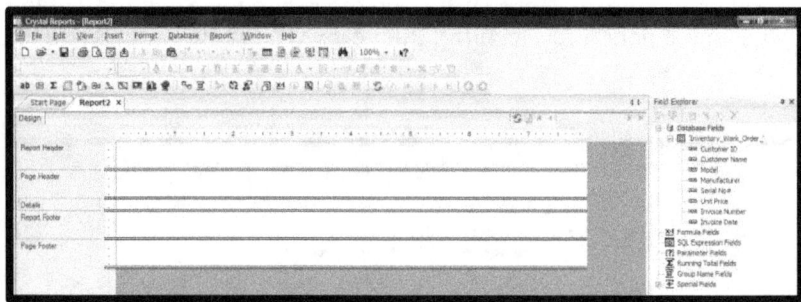

Figure 2.6a – Database Fields

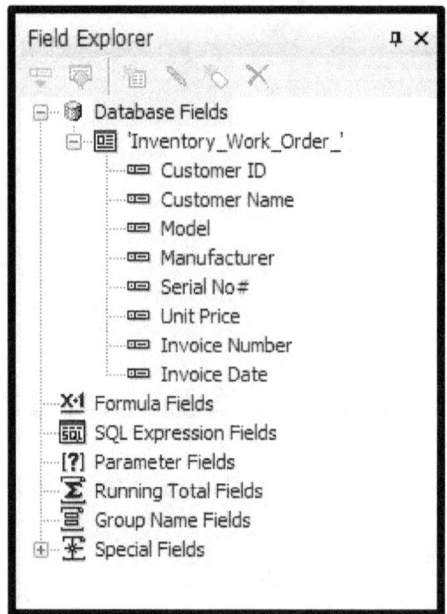

Figure 2.6b – Database Fields

Chapter 2 – DEVELOPING A REPORT

Now, let's do the second connection using **ODBC (RDO)** connection. From Crystal Reports start page, select **File** then **New** and click **Blank Report** or on the start page, just click on Blank Report then expand the **Create New Connection** and **ODBC (RDO)**. Select "**Crystal Reports**" Data source then click "**Next**". On the Database Expert, select inventory Work order table from Crystal Report Database and click the right arrow button to move it to Selected Tables section. As you can see in the Database field from Field Explorer, we now connected to **Inventory Work Order**, as shown below in figure 2.7a, 2.7b, 2.7c, and 2.7d.

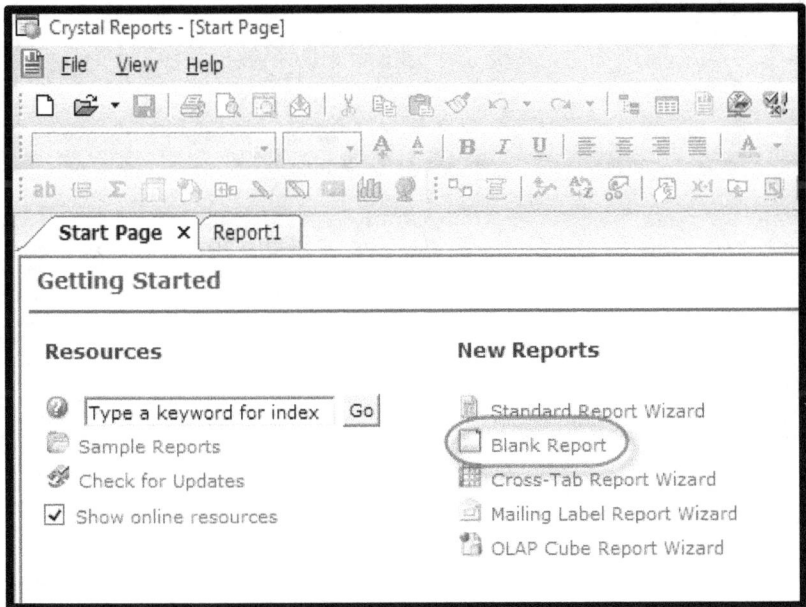

Figure 2.7a - Blank Report from start page

Chapter 2 – DEVELOPING A REPORT

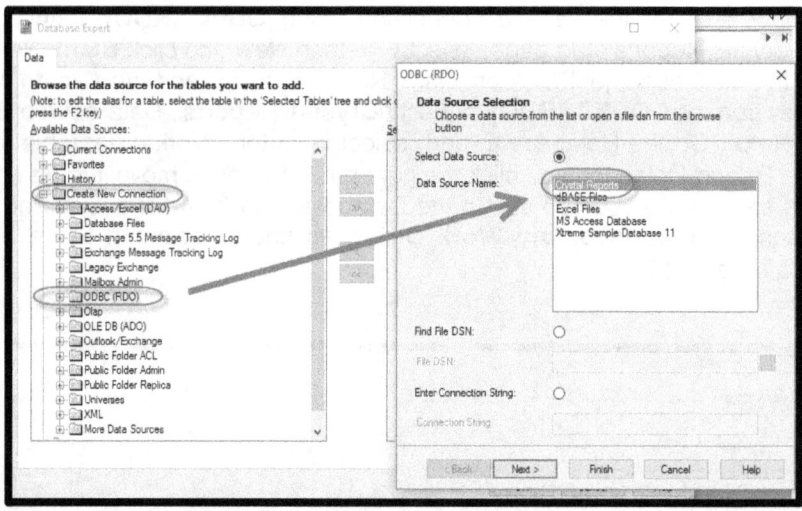

Figure 2.7b – ODBC (RDO) to Crystal Reports Data source for SQL Server

Chapter 2 – DEVELOPING A REPORT

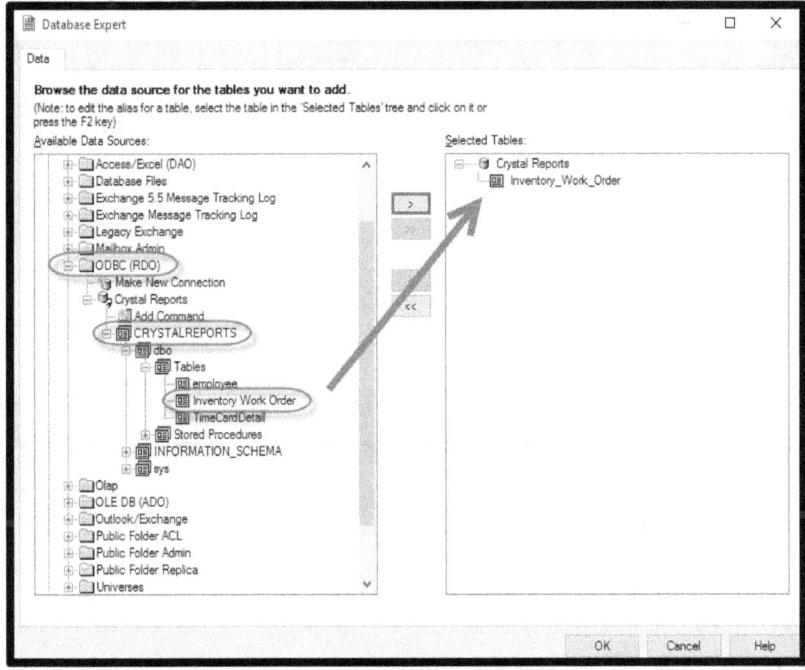

***Figure 2.7c** – Select and move Inventory Work Order table to Selected Tables area*

Chapter 2 – DEVELOPING A REPORT

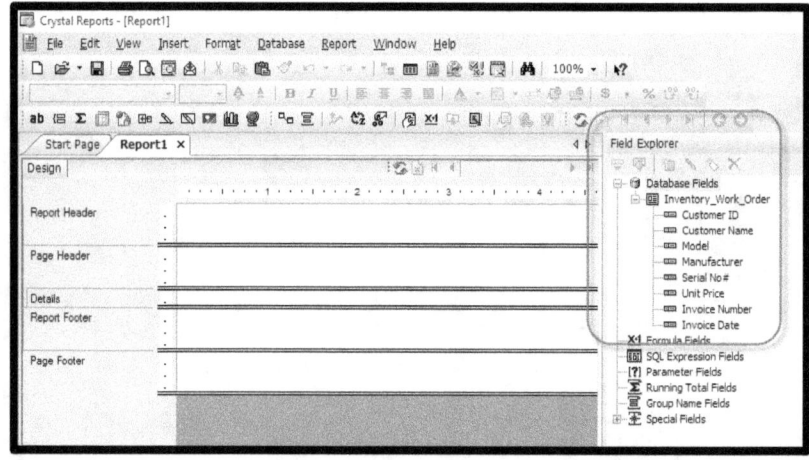

Figure 2.7d – *Connected to Inventory Work Order table from SQL Server*

Setup ODBC Connection

To enable **ODBC** (**RDO**) connection of Crystal Reports data source like what shown in figure 2.7b, you need to setup and add the SQL data source thru the **ODBC** setup administrator from your local computer.

Chapter 2 – DEVELOPING A REPORT

From your local computer, go to **Control Panel** then **Administrative Tools**. Choose either *32-bit* or *64-bit* ODBC setup (depending on your computer), Select "**User DSN**" tab and click "**Add**", as shown below in figure 2.7e and 2.7f.

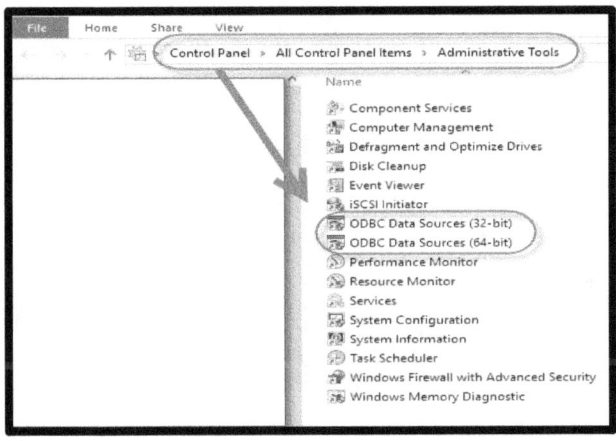

Figure 2.7e – ODBC Administrative from Control Panel

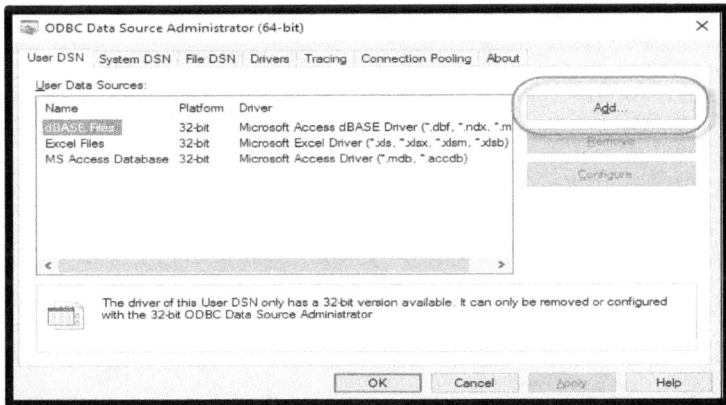

Figure 2.7f – Add the User DSN in ODBC Data Source Administrator

Chapter 2 – DEVELOPING A REPORT

Select "**SQL Server Native Client 11.0**" then clicks "**Finish**" as shown below in figure 2.7g.

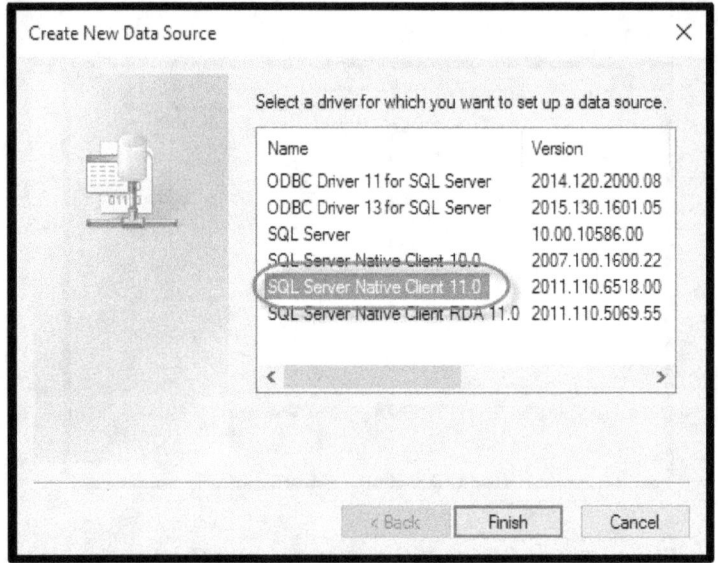

Figure 2.7g – *Select* SQL Server Native Client 11.0

Type the data source name (in this example, **Crystal Reports**) and locate the server you are connecting to, as shown below in figure 2.7h and 2.7i.

Chapter 2 – DEVELOPING A REPORT

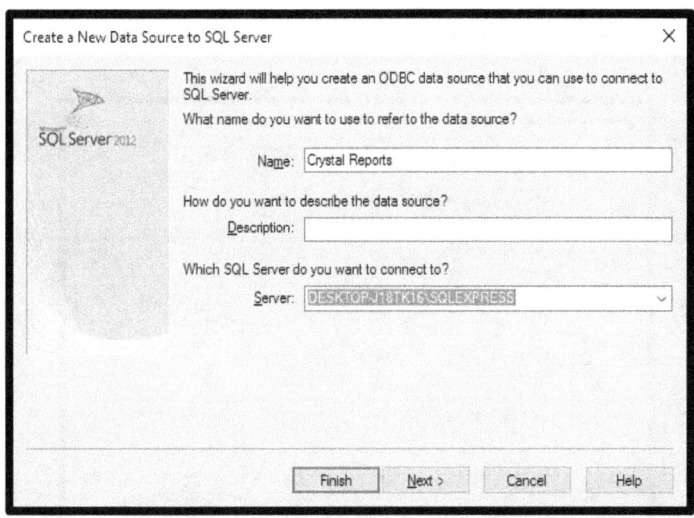

Figure 2.7h – *Type data source and SQL server name*

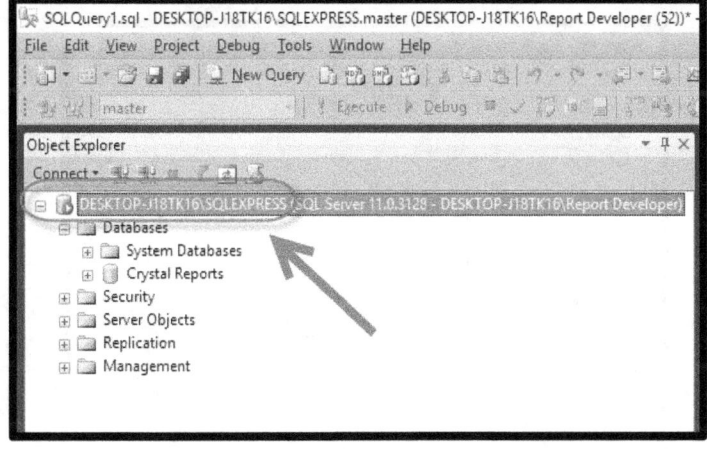

Figure 2.7i – *SQL server name*

Chapter 2 – DEVELOPING A REPORT

Follow default selections below in figure 2.7j, 2.7k, and 2.7l.

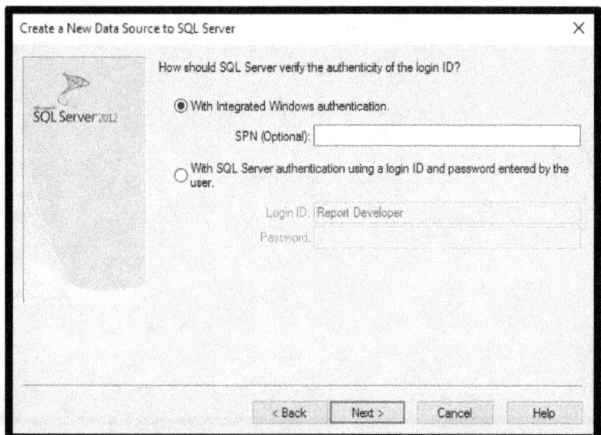

Figure 2.7j – With Integrated Windows authentication

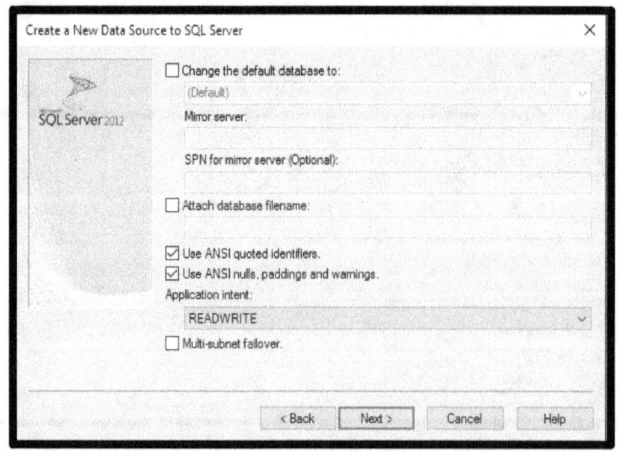

Figure 2.7k – Choose "Use ANSI quoted identifiers" and "Use ANSI nulls, paddings and warnings" and select "READWHITE" of Application Intent.

Chapter 2 – DEVELOPING A REPORT

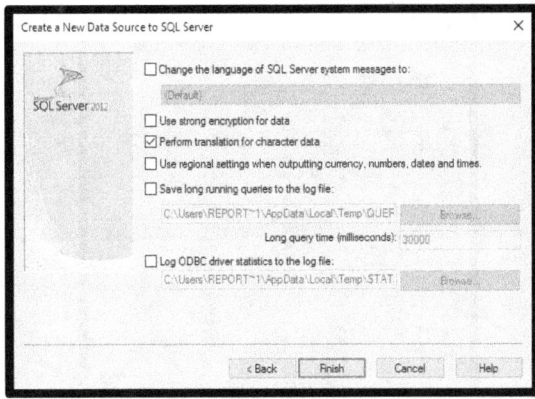

Figure 2.7l – Perform transaction for character data

Click "**Test Data Source**" to test the connection setup then click **OK** to complete the setup as show below in figure 2.7m and 2.7n.

Figure 2.7m – Test Data Source

Chapter 2 – DEVELOPING A REPORT

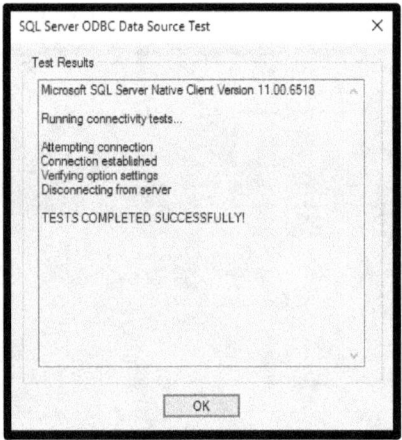

Figure 2.7n – Test completed successfully!

Congratulations, the Crystal Reports data source is now registered in the **ODBC** data source administrator setup! See below in figure 2.7o.

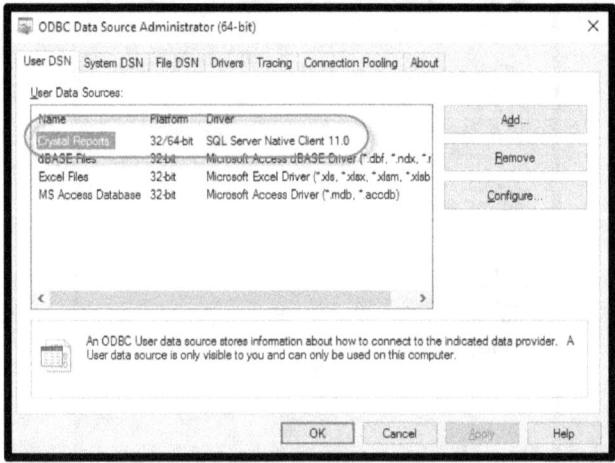

Figure 2.7n – Crystal Reports data source is now registered in the ODBC data source administrator

Chapter 2 – DEVELOPING A REPORT

Create a New Report

Congratulations! You just learned how to connect to the data source thru "**Create New Connection**", and got all the data ready for a new report. Now let's continue, using all the data from the **Inventory_Work_Order_** spreadsheet in the **Database Fields**.

Click and drag each column of the **Inventory_Work_Order_** file from the **Field Explorer** to the **Details** domain of the **Design** view, as shown below in figure 2.8a. *Crystal Reports* will automatically generate the header for each table that you drag into the **Details** field. If you need to rename the text object header, simply just double click it.

You also have the option to delete and create a new text object by using the "**Insert - Text Object".** To insert a new text object, choose "**Insert Text Object**" icon, then click on the report header areas, as shown in below figure 2.8b.

Chapter 2 – DEVELOPING A REPORT

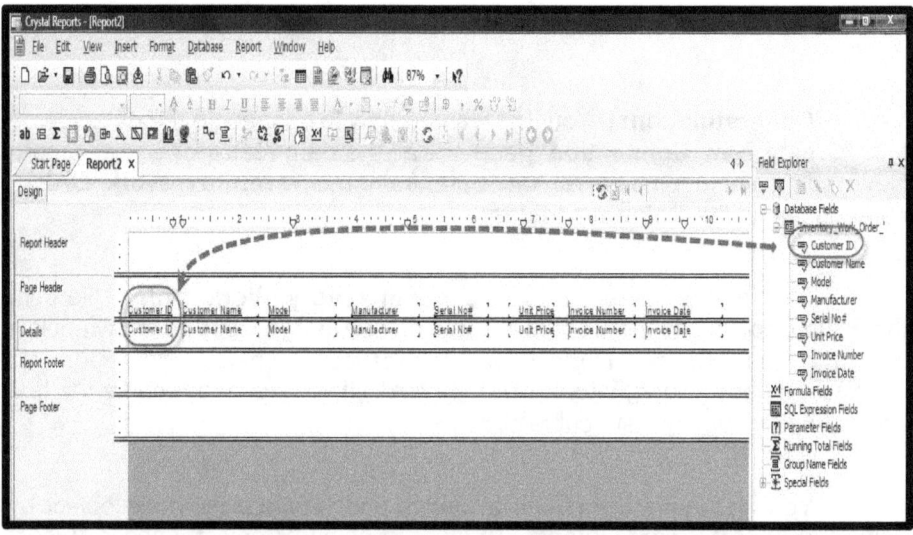

Figure 2.8a – Click and drag the Inventory_Work_Order_ column into Details on the Design's fields

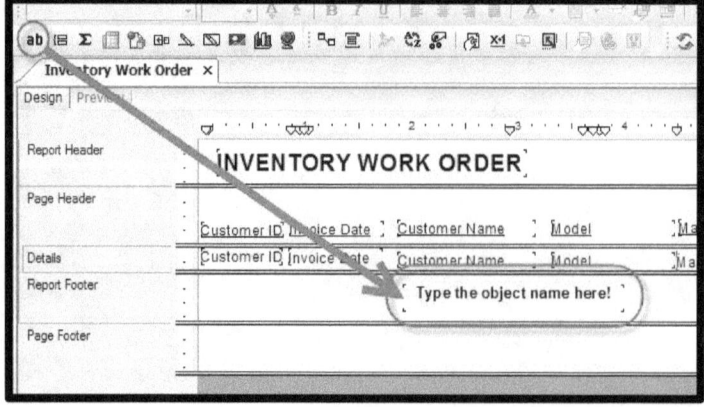

Figure 2.8b – Using Text Object icon to insert a new text box object

Chapter 2 – DEVELOPING A REPORT

Now, if you look carefully in the **Field Explorer**, you can see that each column in the "**Inventory_Work_Order_**" data file (**Customer ID**, **Customer Name**, **Model**, **Manufacturer**, **Serial No#**, **Unit Price**, **Invoice Number**, and **Invoice Date**) has a green check mark under the icon. The green check mark means that the column has been pulled from **Field Explorer**, and placed in a **Design's** Report field (**active**), as shown below in figure 2.9.

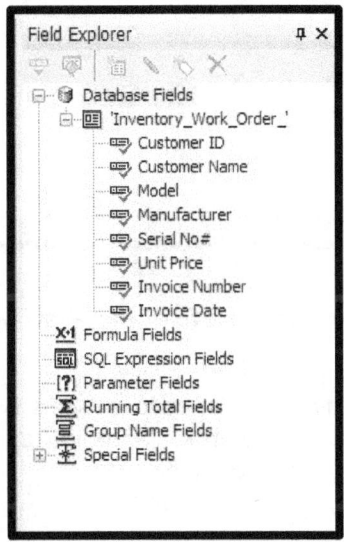

Figure 2.9 – *The green check mark will appear next to a column if that column was placed onto the Design Report fields.*

Now, let's preview the report. Open the **View** menu and click **Print Preview,** as shown below in figure 2.10.

Chapter 2 – DEVELOPING A REPORT

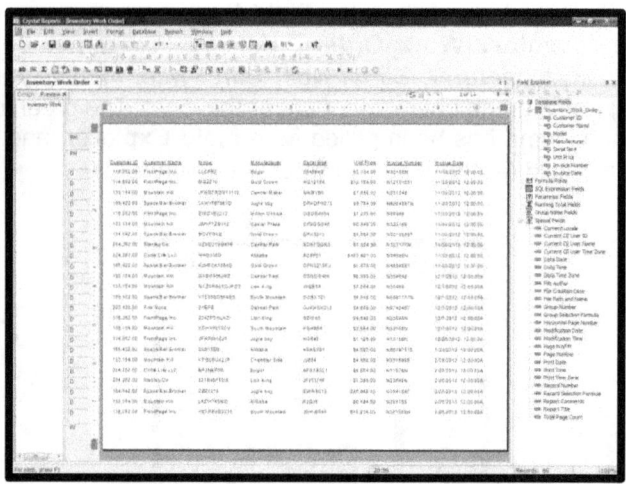

Figure 2.10 – *Print Preview*

The report is not finished yet because we still need to add a **Header** (every report needs a Header), and add an object(s) such as *Page Number* on the **Page Footer** field. Let's continue.

Insert Text Object

Switch back from the **Preview Tab** to the **Design Tab**. Go to the **Insert** menu and click **Text Object**. You will see the (**+**) cursor sign. Click the **Header** area and type **Inventory Work Order** inside the Text Object box, as shown below in figure 2.11a and 2.11b.

Chapter 2 – DEVELOPING A REPORT

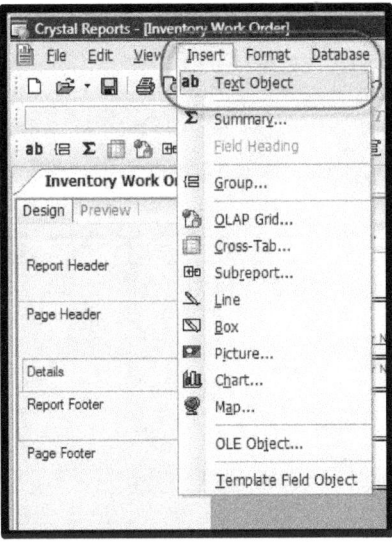

Figure 2.11a – *Insert Text Object*

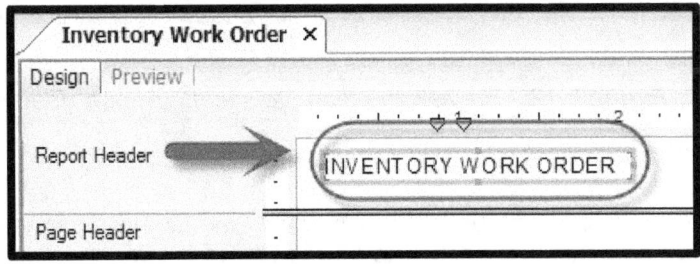

Figure 2.11b – *Type Inventory Work Order inside the Text Object box*

Examine your work by clicking on the **Preview** tab. Your report header should look like the one illustrated below, as shown below in figure 2.12.

Chapter 2 – DEVELOPING A REPORT

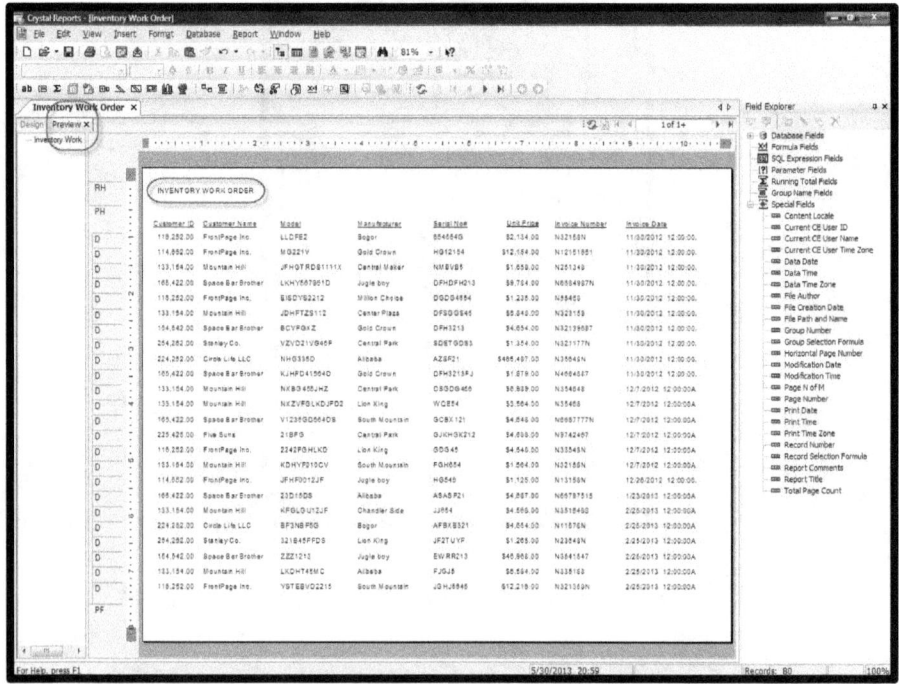

Figure 2.12 – Preview the report to see the Report Header

For multiple page reports, you'll probably want to have page numbers. Let's add a Page Number function to the bottom of our report page. Switch from the **Preview** Tab back to the **Design** Tab, and then Click and drag a field called **Page N of M** from **Special Fields** in the **Field Explorer**. Drop the object onto the Design's Reports **Page Footer** field, as shown below in figure 2.13.

Chapter 2 – DEVELOPING A REPORT

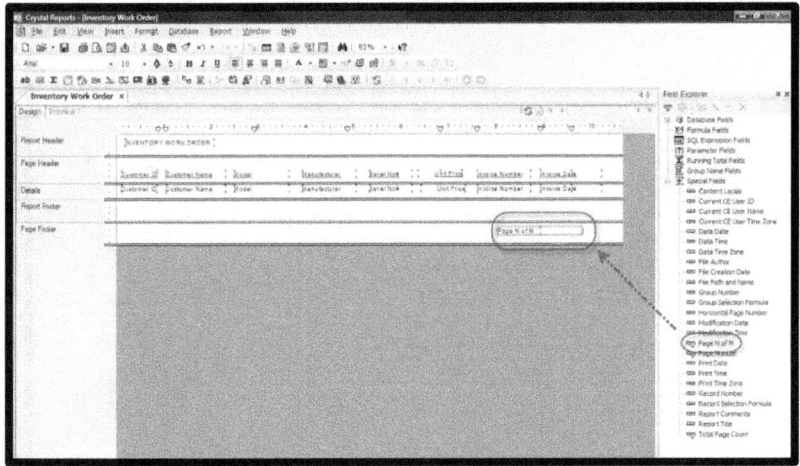

Figure 2.13 – *Add Page N of M to the Page Footer*

Let's preview the report again and **CONGRATULATIONS**! You have created a basic report using *Crystal Reports* and an Excel Spreadsheet as a data source connection, as shown below in figure 2.14.

Chapter 2 – DEVELOPING A REPORT

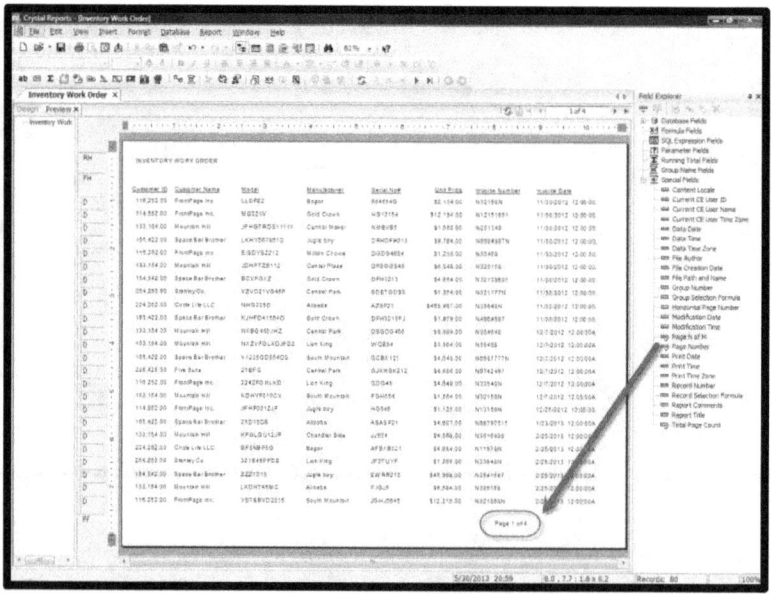

Figure 2.14 – Preview the report to check Page Number field

> **Note:** In the Special Fields, if you choose **Page N of M**, the **Page Number**, **Page N of M** and **Total Page Count** Icons will all get a green check mark, but if you choose **Page Number,** only that field will get the check mark. The reason for this is that the **Page N of M** function activates other numbering functions besides just itself, while the **Page Number** function acts alone.

Great! You now know how to use **Crystal Reports** to display data from an **Excel** file! Very useful, but don't stop now, you're just getting started. The data is all there, but so far it doesn't look like much. Let's see if we can add a little style and life in the next chapter to the report to make it an attention better!

Chapter 3 – FORMATTING A REPORT

To make a visually appealing presentation with *Crystal Reports*, you will need to know how to do formatting. Good formatting will make your report attractive, meaningful, and easy to follow. There are four methods of formatting in *Crystal Reports*, each of which has a unique purpose. These four options are: Formatting Toolbar, Format Field, Select Expert, and Section Expert.

Formatting Toolbar

With **Formatting Toolbar** you have quick access to change the selected fields' *Font face, Increase or Decrease Font Size, change the alignment, add Bold, Italic, Underline, percent, Increase or Decrease Decimal,* etc.

Now, let's open the Inventory Work Order report and make some changes using the **Formatting Toolbar**. The **Formatting Toolbar** will be grayed out (passive) if no fields on the report are selected, as shown below in figure *3.0*.

Chapter 3 – FORMATTING A REPORT

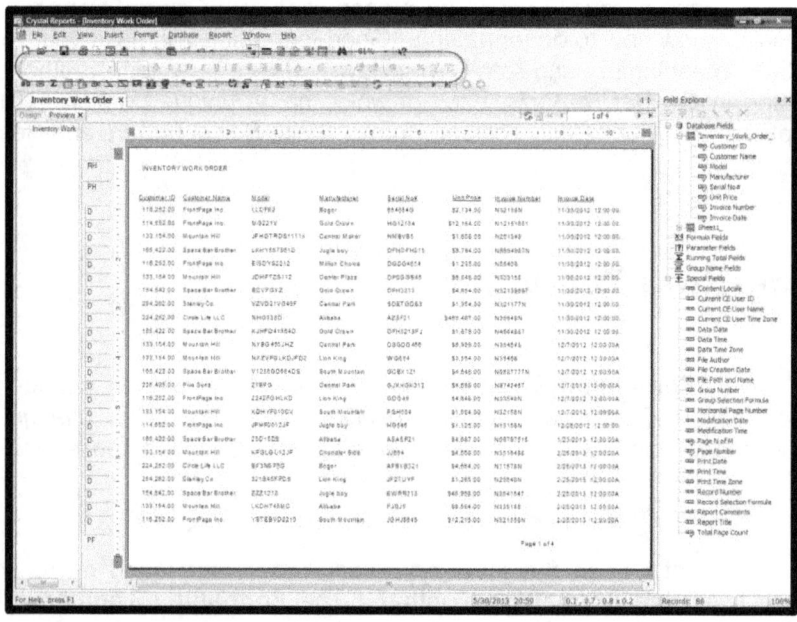

Figure 3.0 – *The Formatting Toolbar is grayed out (passive) because none of the fields on report have been selected.*

Format changes can be made in either **Design Tab** or **Preview Tab**. I prefer to do them in the **Preview Tab** because I can see how the changes will look on the printed page as soon as they are entered.

In the **Preview Tab**, select the title **"Inventory Work Order"** located on the **Report Header**. Once a field is selected, the Formatting toolbar becomes active. Notice that a little rectangular blue box appeared on the words **"Inventory Work Order"**. This is the measurement for the field's **Object size and position**. To activate the **Object Size and Position**, just right click on the selected field, and then click "**Size and Position**", as shown below in figure *3.1a, 3.1b, and 3.1c.*

Chapter 3 – FORMATTING A REPORT

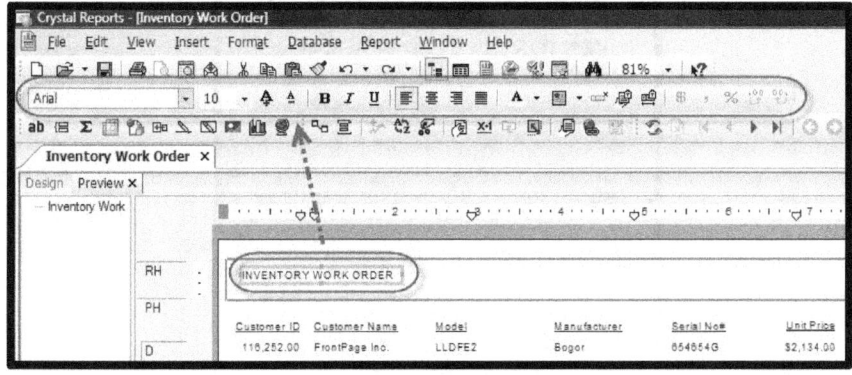

Figure 3.1a – *The Formatting toolbar is active once a word or object is selected.*

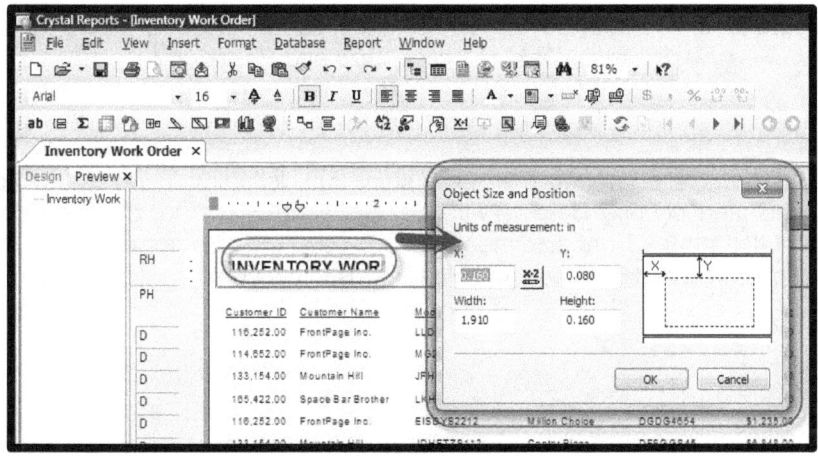

Figure 3.1b – *Object Size and Position of a field appear as a blue rectangular box.*

Chapter 3 – FORMATTING A REPORT

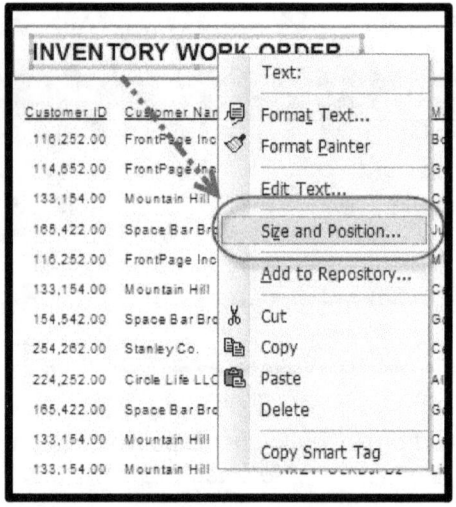

Figure 3.1c – *To activate Object Size and Position, just right click on the selection field and click "Size and Position".*

To make our report title really stand out, let's first increase the **Font** size, and then choose **Bold**. With the title words selected, click the down arrow button on the **Font** size menu and increase the size from **10** to **16**, and then click **B** or (**Ctrl+B**) to bold the **Header**, as shown below in figure *3.1d*.

Chapter 3 – FORMATTING A REPORT

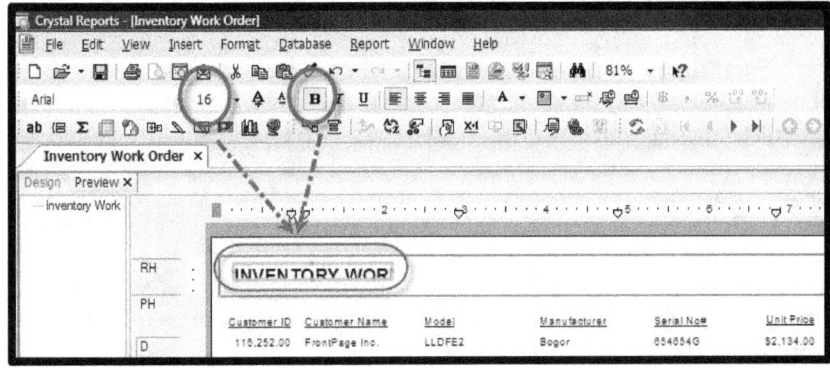

Figure 3.1d – *Increase the Font size and bold the header.*

You will notice that when you increase the font size, the highlighted phrase no longer fits inside the blue rectangle. To expand the rectangle so the header can be read without cutting off the text, simply right click on the selected field, click **Size and Position**, then set (*in this example*) **Width: 3.00** and **Height:0.25**, as shown below in figure *3.1e*.

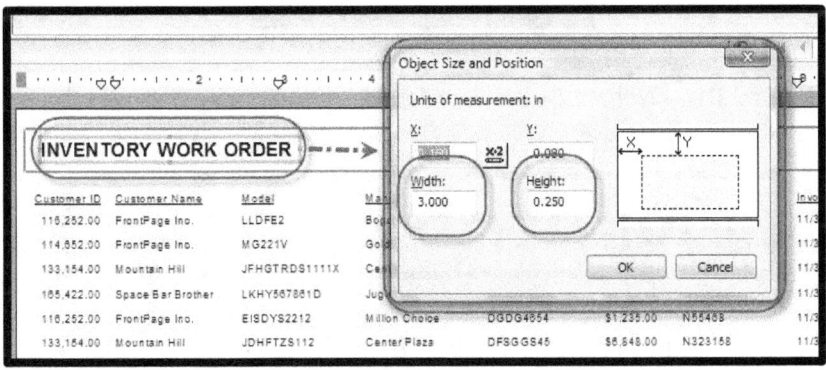

Figure 3.1e – *Set the Width and Height properties of the header title object so it can be read without truncating the text.*

Chapter 3 – FORMATTING A REPORT

> **Note:** There is a quick way to set the **Object size and Position**. The "blue" rectangle box (*blue in your Crystal Report but black on this book*) has a dot (called a handle) on each corner and at the mid-point of each side. To resize the object, just grab a handle with the cursor, and drag the box to the correct size. Grabbing a mid-point allows you to stretch in a direction perpendicular to the side selected; grabbing the corner handle lets you change the overall size of the box while maintaining the original aspect ratio, as shown below in figure *3.1f, 3.1g, and 3.1h*.
>
> *Press and hold on "ALT" key will unlock the movement of the field(s) so you can resize to the exact position you want when you resizing or moving the field.*

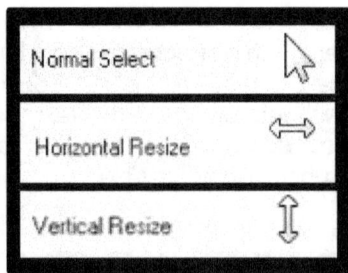

Figure 3.1f – Normal Select, Horizontal, and Vertical Resize cursors.

Figure 3.1g – the "blue" dots (handles) to resize the Object Size and Position.

Reporting With Visual Crystal Reports

Chapter 3 – FORMATTING A REPORT

INVENTORY WORK ORDER

Figure 3.1h – *The Inventory Work Order header after resizing.*

Notes:

Figure 3.1i below shows the **Object Size and Position** properties of the **Inventory Work Order** object.

X – The left size and position between the row gray box and the object box (Inventory Work Order)

Y – The top size and position between the row gray box and the object box (Inventory Work Order)

Width – The width size and position of the object (Inventory Work Order)

Height – The height size and position of the object (Inventory Work Order)

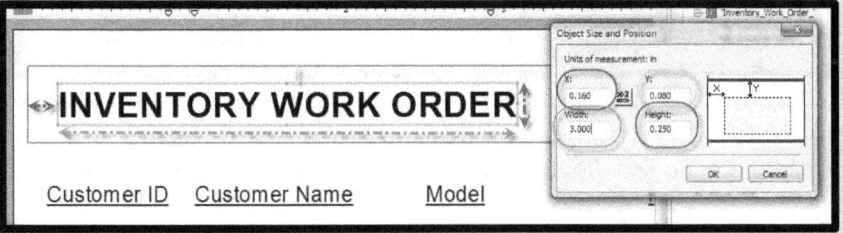

Figure 3.1i – *The Size and Position properties of the Inventory Work Order object.*

Chapter 3 – FORMATTING A REPORT

There are eight columns of data in the **Page Header** fields. Let's change the column headers to make them stand out from the rest of the data. Since all of the headers will have the same format, you can change them all simultaneously by doing the following:

- Click on the first Header, **Customer ID**, hold down the **Ctrl** key on your keyboard, and then select each of the remaining headers one by one until they are all highlighted.

- When all of the Headers are selected, click **B** on the Formatting toolbar, or use the hotkeys **Ctrl+B,** to change all of the Headers to **bold** font , as shown below in figure *3.2a and 3.2b*.

Figure 3.2a – *To format all the Headers at the same time, select the first Header, hold down the Ctrl key, select the next Header, and so on.*

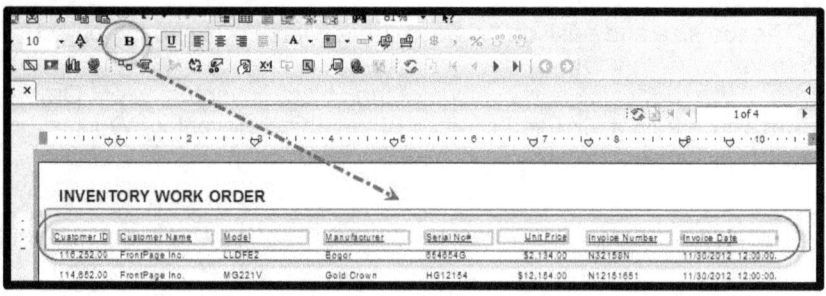

Figure 3.2b – *Each Column Header is bold.*

Chapter 3 – FORMATTING A REPORT

Field Formatting

Since each column of data represents something different, they will not all be formatted the same way. Crystal Reports has a wide range of built-in format styles that can quickly be applied to your data tables. For example, if our column of data represents numeric values, we can select the level of precision to range anywhere from whole numbers to eight or more decimal places. We can also define and display data as text, currency, dates, custom format, etc.

If we look at our **Inventory Work Order** report, we will see a column for **Customer ID**. The default setting for this field is commas and decimals. We want the **Customer ID** to be a plain integer, so we will change it. We also want to change the date display in the **Invoice Date** column to show the date only, and not the time, as shown below in figure *3.3a*.

Customer ID	Customer Name	Model	Manufacturer	Serial No#	Unit Price	Invoice Number	Invoice Date
116,252.00	FrontPage Inc.	LLDFE2	Boger	654654G	$2,134.00	N32158N	11/30/2012 12:00:00AM
114,652.00	FrontPage Inc.	MG221V	Gold Crown	HG12154	$12,154.00	N12151651	11/30/2012 12:00:00AM
133,154.00	Mountain Hill	JFHGTRDS1111X	Central Maker	NMBVB5	$1,858.00	N251348	11/30/2012 12:00:00AM
165,422.00	Space Bar Brother	LKHY567851D	Jugle boy	DFHDFH213	$9,784.00	N6684957N	11/30/2012 12:00:00AM

***Figure 3.3a** – Use Format field to do the report formatting on Customer ID and Invoice Date*

Right click on one of the **Customer ID** details, and then select Format Field, as shown below in figure *3.3b*.

Chapter 3 – FORMATTING A REPORT

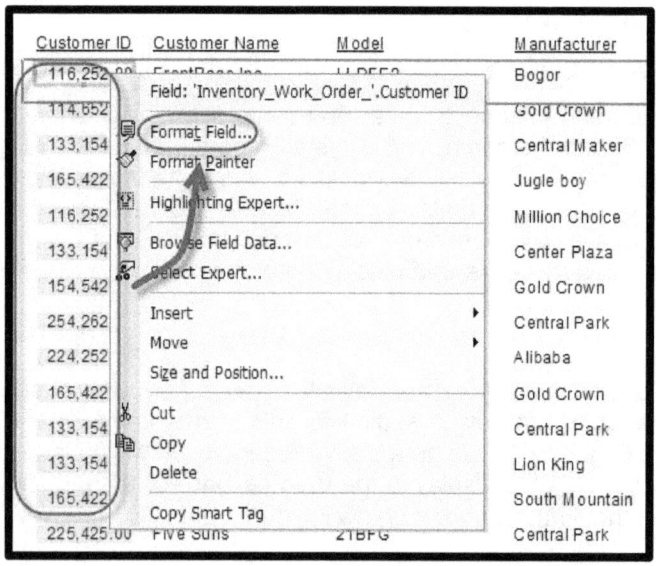

Figure 3.3b – Right click on one of the Customer ID's Details and Select Format Field

On the **Format Editor**, make sure the **Number Tab** is selected, choose **(1123),** and then click **OK**, as shown below in figure *3.3c and 3.3d.*

Chapter 3 – FORMATTING A REPORT

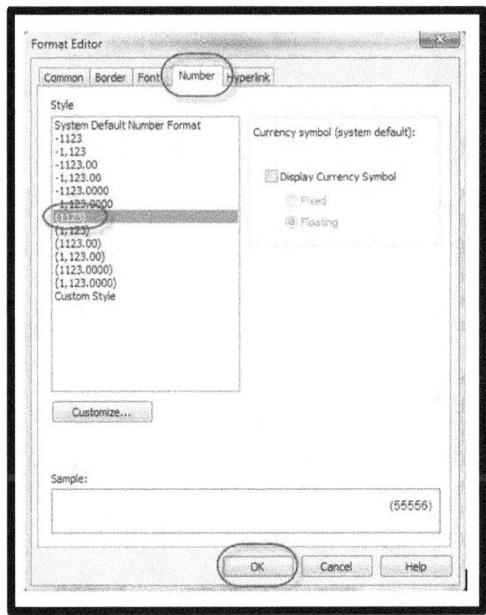

Figure 3.3c – On the Format Editor, select Number Tab, then select (1123) and click OK.

Chapter 3 – FORMATTING A REPORT

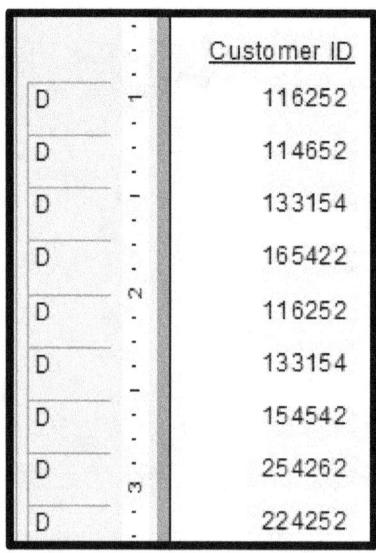

Figure 3.3d – *Customer ID format set as numbers only.*

In our data table, the column labeled Invoice Date shows dates and times. We don't need to know the transaction times, and they take up space on our form, so let's change the format to only display the date. Right click on **Invoice Date,** and then Select **Format Field**, as shown below in figure *3.4a*.

Chapter 3 – FORMATTING A REPORT

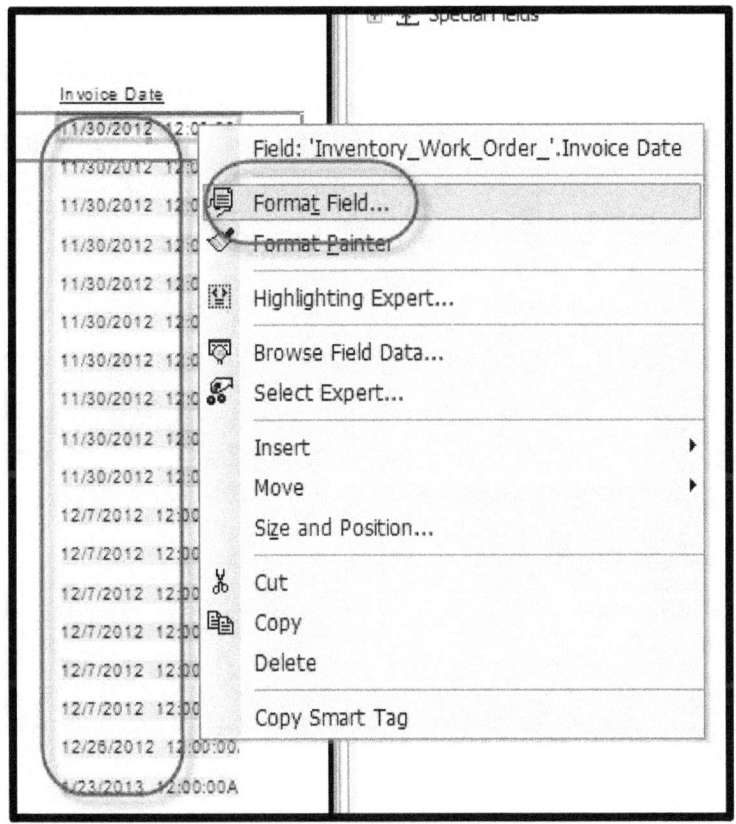

Figure 3.4a – *Right click on Invoice Date, and then select Format Field.*

On the **Format Editor**, select the **Date and Time** tab, and then, from among the many options provided, choose "**03/01/1999**", as shown below in figure *3.4b*.

Chapter 3 – FORMATTING A REPORT

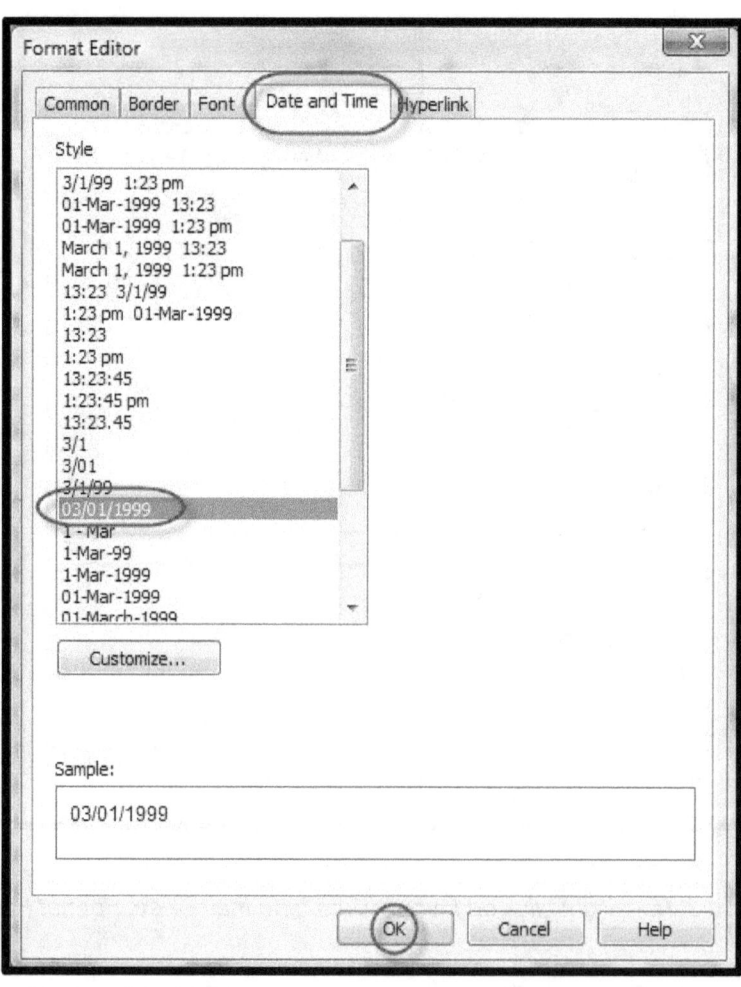

Figure 3.4b – *On Format Editor, click on the Date and Time tab, and then select 03/01/1999.*

Chapter 3 – FORMATTING A REPORT

The dates in your table should now look like this, as shown below in figure 3.4c.

Invoice Date
11/30/2012
11/30/2012
11/30/2012
11/30/2012
11/30/2012
11/30/2012
11/30/2012
11/30/2012
11/30/2012
11/30/2012
12/07/2012
12/07/2012

Figure 3.4c – *Date format of Invoice Date changed to date only without time*

Chapter 3 – FORMATTING A REPORT

Format Editor

When you format a field, the **Format Editor** will appear and allow you to perform other formatting options such as **Common**, **Border**, **Font**, **Paragraph** and **Hyperlink**. Let's take a quick look at how those features work.

Common Tab

Please see figure 3.5 for the **Common tab**.

Figure 3.5 – *Common tab of the Format Editor*

Chapter 3 – FORMATTING A REPORT

- **Object Name**–This option displays name of the object you have selected. You can keep the default, or change it here, as shown below in figure 3.6.

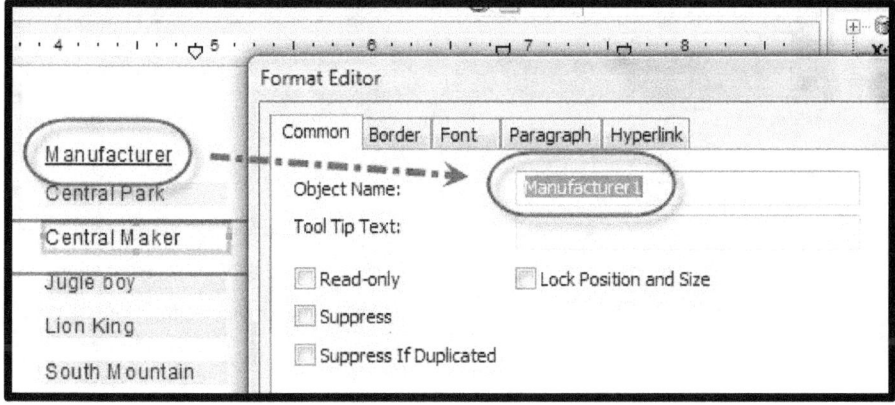

Figure 3.6 – *Object Name in Common Tab of Format Editor.*

- **Tool Tip Text** – Have you ever seen those little help prompts that sometimes appear when you hover your cursor over a screen object? This is where you can create and apply them to objects in your form, as shown below in figure *3.7a and 3.7b*.

Chapter 3 – FORMATTING A REPORT

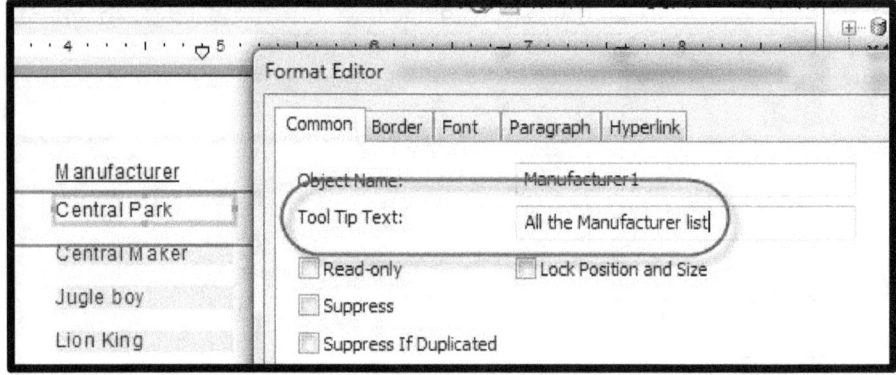

Figure 3.7a – *Tool Tip Text in Common Tab in Format Editor.*

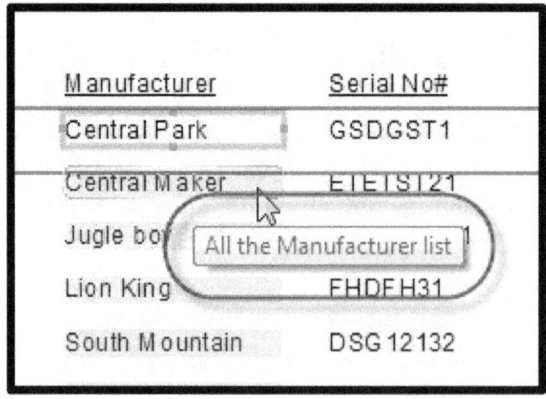

Figure 3.7b – *The text bubble appears when you hover over the report fields.*

Chapter 3 – FORMATTING A REPORT

- **Read-Only** – This option will lock the field from any formatting except "**Repeat Horizontal Pages**" and "**Lock Position and Size**".

- **Lock Position and Size** – This option locks the position of the selected report object so it cannot be moved or resized.

- **Suppress** – This option enables suppression of the selected object when previewing and printing. When you suppress an object, you prevent it from appearing. The next button, **X+2** ( ) is a useful option to allow suppression based on criteria or conditions. For example, we may want to suppress the Manufacturer field on all pages except page 1. To do this, select the field you want to suppress, click on the **X+2** button, and type "*pagenumber > 1*" into the **Formula Workshop – Format Formula Editor.** This will suppress the selected field everywhere except on page 1, as shown below in figure *3.8*.

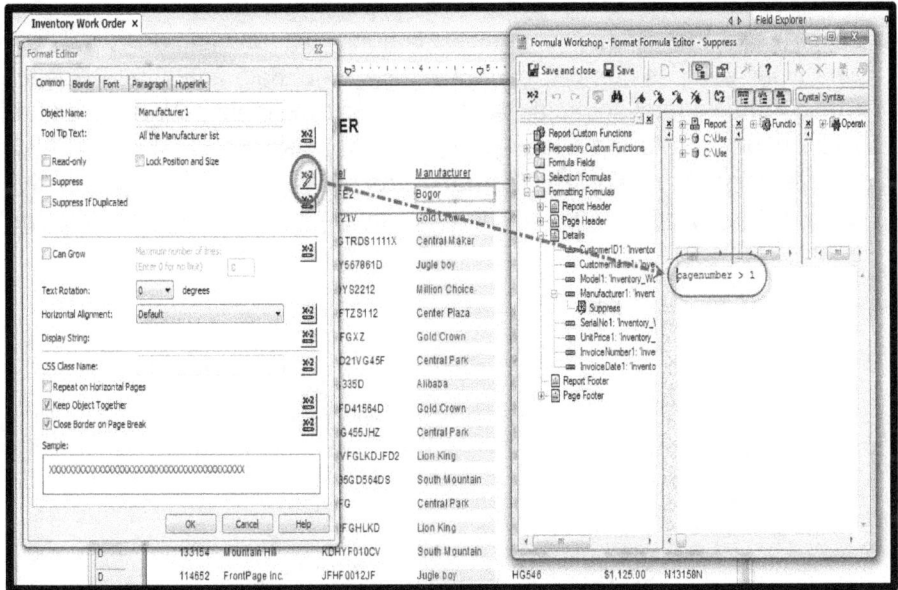

Figure 3.8 – Suppress option in Common Tab in the Format Editor

Chapter 3 – FORMATTING A REPORT

> **Note:** The **X+2** button color will change from blue to red when there is a formula in the Formula Workshop.

- **Suppress If Duplicated** – This option enables suppression of repeated field names on the report.

- **Can Grow**–This option enables variable length fields to grow vertically [|] (*up and down*) on the report with auto word wrap.

- **Text Rotation** – This option allows text rotation.

- **Horizontal Alignment** – This option allows the field horizontal alignment to be set by default, left, right, center, and justified.

- **Display String** – This option enables conditional formatting and display of field types such as number, currency, date, time, date and time, Boolean, String, running total, formulas, and so on (See example below). Click the **X+2** button next to the **Display String** and insert this formula: "**UCASE ({'*Inventory_Work_Order_*'.*Manufacturer*})**" This will change all the Manufacturer fields to upper case, as shown below in figure *3.9a and 3.9b*.

Chapter 3 – FORMATTING A REPORT

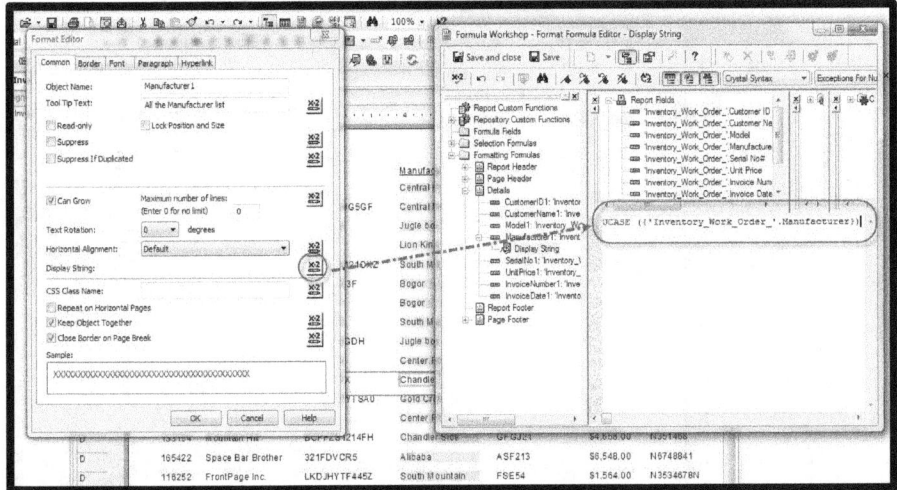

Figure 3.9a – Display String to change all the Manufacturer fields to upper case

Chapter 3 – FORMATTING A REPORT

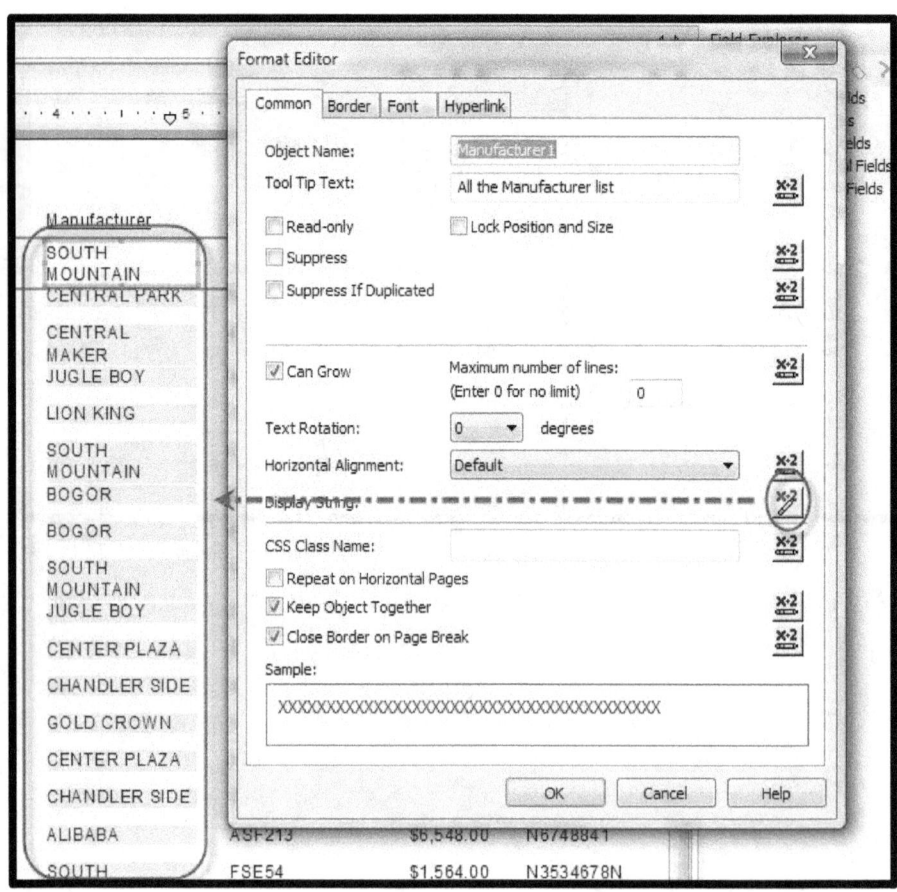

Figure 3.9b – *All the Manufacturer fields are now in upper case*

- **CSS Class Name**—Choosing this option lets you leverage the existing Cascading Style Sheet to format report fields over the web application, or with Business Object Enterprises. So, when a report is rendered and viewed over the Web, the formatting options are automatically converted to HTML (for web application).

Chapter 3 – FORMATTING A REPORT

- **Repeat on Horizontal Pages** - This option enables the repetition of specified fields across horizontal page breaks. This option will be useful to keep the horizontal page print on all pages when the report has multiple pages like a crosstab chart.

- **Keep Object Together** – This option keeps an object on a single page. However, if there not enough space, the object will print or display on the next page. Basically, this is an option to prevent image breaking across pages.

- **Close Border on Page Break** – Choosing this option makes sure that the printed field on each page has a full border around all the partial text.

Border Tab

Please see figure 3.10 for the **Border tab.**

Chapter 3 – FORMATTING A REPORT

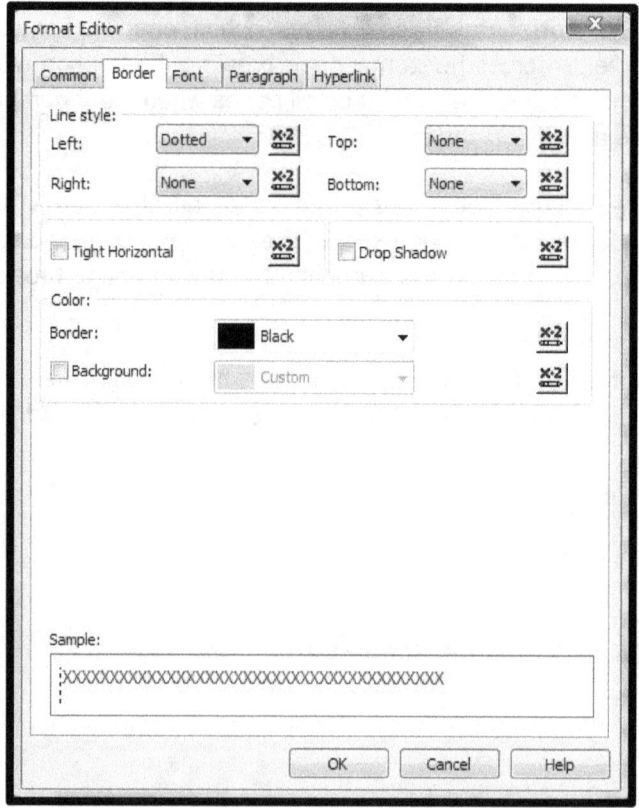

Figure 3.10 – Border tab of the Format Editor

- **Line Style** – Use this option to set the Left, Right, Top and Bottom borders of a field using different types of supported borders in the drop down boxes such as Single, Double, Dashed, or Dotted.

- **Tight Horizontal** – This option forces object border to wrap tightly around the selection, as shown below in figure 3.11a and 3.11b before and after using this option.

Chapter 3 – FORMATTING A REPORT

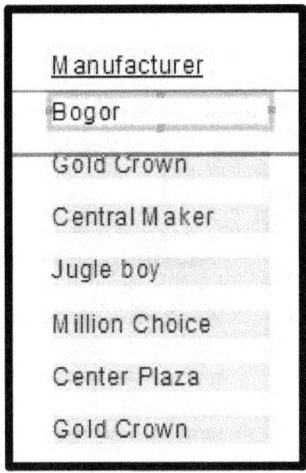

Figure 3.11a – *Before using Tight Horizontal.*

Figure 3.11b – *After using Tight Horizontal.*

Chapter 3 – FORMATTING A REPORT

- **Drop Shadow** – This option displays shadows behind objects to give them dimensional perspective, as shown below in figure 3.12.

Figure 3.12 – *Drop Shadow option of the Border tab*

- **Border** – This option will set the border's line color. The Drop Shadow color specification is specified in this option.

- **Background** – This option will set the background color of the object, as shown below in figure 3.13.

Chapter 3 – FORMATTING A REPORT

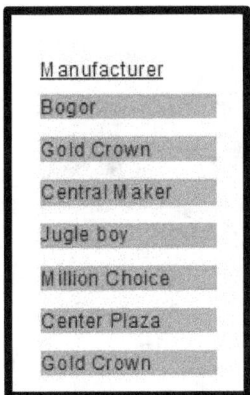

Figure 3.13 – *Set the Background color of text objects*

Font Tab

Please see figure 3.14 for the **Font tab**.

Chapter 3 – FORMATTING A REPORT

Figure 3.14 – *Font tab of the Format Editor*

The options in the Font tab of the Format Editor allow you to change the fonts, font size and font style for text and data fields.

- **Font, Style, Size and Color**–This option allows selection of a variety of font types such as Arial, Calibri, and Times Roman, text styles such as bold and Italic, and colors.

- **Strikeout and Underline** – This option allows underlines and strikeouts on the current report object.

Chapter 3 – FORMATTING A REPORT

- **Character Spacing Exactly** – This option will allow you to specify the space that each character in the selected font occupies. The default character spacing is 0 pts. For example if you specify a 12 point font with character spacing of 12 points, each character will remain as a 12 point font size, occupying a space that is 12 point wide, as shown below in figure *3.15a, 3.15b and 3.15c*.

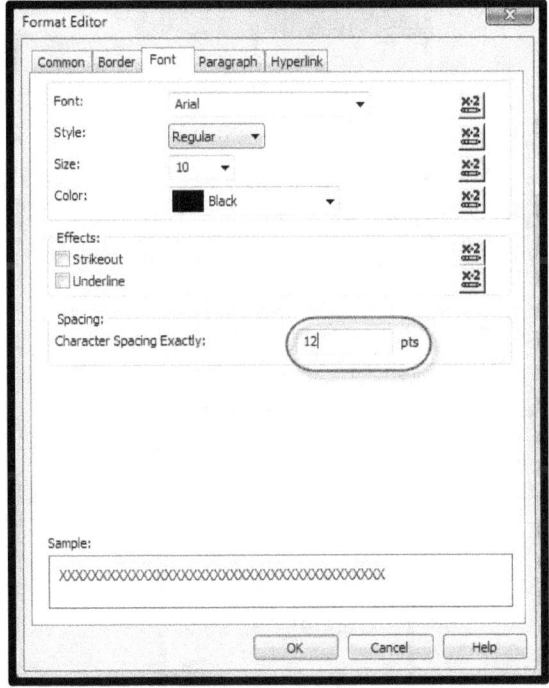

Figure 3.15a – *Set the character spacing to 12 in Font tab of the Format Editor*

Chapter 3 – FORMATTING A REPORT

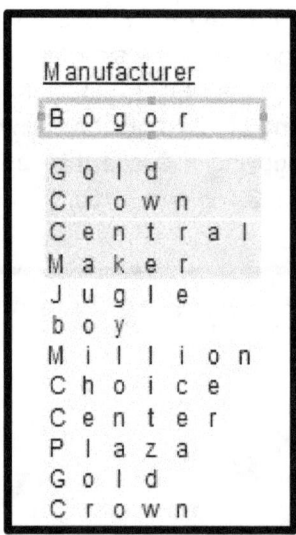

Figure 3.15b – Font character spacing has been set to 12

Figure 3.15c – Default character spacing with 0 pts

Chapter 3 – FORMATTING A REPORT

Paragraph Tab

Please see figure 3.16 for the **Paragraph tab**.

Figure 3.16 - Paragraph tab in the Format Editor. Reading order from left to right is the default.

Chapter 3 – FORMATTING A REPORT

- **First Line** – This option allows you to define the indent distance of the first line of a paragraph in inches (between 0 and 1.16).

- **Left** – This option allows you to define the left margin distance in inches (between 0 and 1.16).

- **Right** – This option allows you to define the right margin distance in inches (between 0 and 1.16).

- **Line Spacing** – This option allows you to enter the spacing between lines as a multiple of the font size or as an exact number of points.
- **Of** – This option lets you define line spacing distance as a multiple of normal. Normal is defined as single space, or a ratio of 1 to 1. Adjust the line spacing by entering a value greater than or less than 1 (negative numbers not allowed).

- **Left to Right** – This option will set the system to read the text from left to right. This is the default setting.

- **Right to Left** – This option will set the system to read the text from right to left.

- **Text Interpretation** – Sets the format of imported text fields.

    o **None** – This option will set the text read as a plain text
    o **RTF** – This option will set the text read as Rich Text Format or RTF
    o **HTML**–This option will set the text read as Hyper Text Markup Language or HTML data

Chapter 3 – FORMATTING A REPORT

Hyperlink Tab

Please see figure 3.17 for the **Hyperlink tab**.

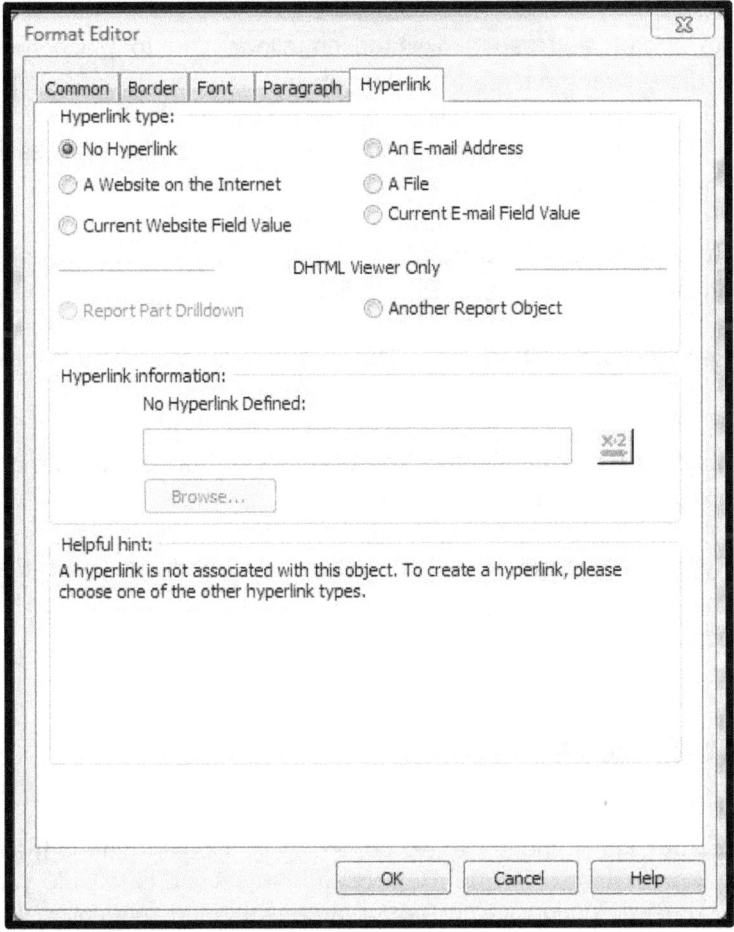

Figure 3.17 - *Hyperlink tab in the Format Editor*

Chapter 3 – FORMATTING A REPORT

- **No Hyperlink** – This default option will suppress **Hyperlink**.

- **A Website on the Internet** – Choosing this option allows you to place the website address over the Hyperlink Information.

- **Current Website Field Value** – This option will turn the selected field on the report into a website hyperlink.

- **An Email Address** – This option allows you to place the email address over the Hyperlink Information.

- **A File** – This option allows you to point to a file that is accessible for users of the report in the share location.

- **Current E-mail Field Value** – This option will turn the selected field on the report into an e-mail hyperlink.

- **Report Part Drilldown** – This option will allow you to navigate between objects within a report.

- **Another Report Object**– This option allows you to navigate between objects within one or more reports.

- **Hyperlink Information**–This option will be activated if the user chooses any of the options in Hyperlink Type except the No Hyperlink option.

Select Expert

In **Select Expert**, there are two options to filter data. One is the default filter drop down list from **Crystal Report** and the second is to write your own formula. The last option is the most powerful method, and often the only method, to get the results you want.

Chapter 3 – FORMATTING A REPORT

Please see figures 3.18a and 3.18b for the **Select Expert**.

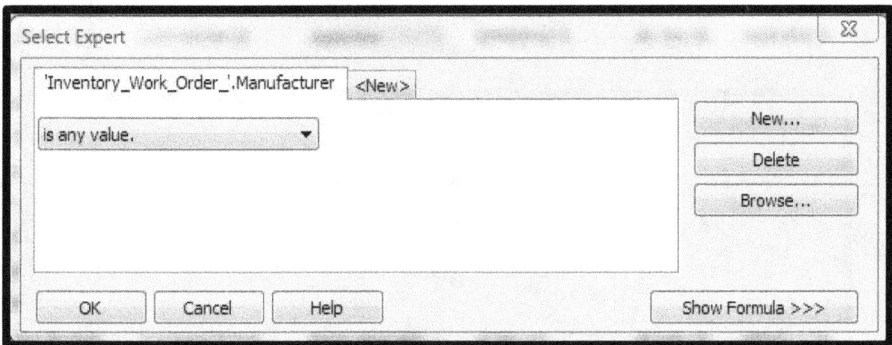

Figure 3.18a – *Select Expert*

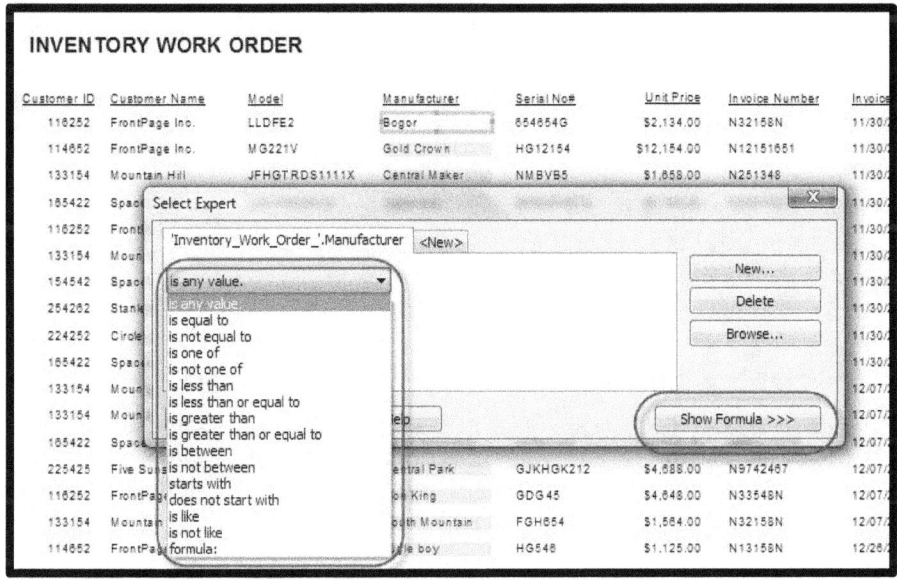

Figure 3.18b – *Choosing from the drop down list or writing the Formula are the two options to filter the data in Select Expert.*

Chapter 3 – FORMATTING A REPORT

Let's do some exercises to filter the data using the **Select Expert**.

Right click on one of the Manufacturer's fields and choose **Select Expert**, as shown below in figure 3.19.

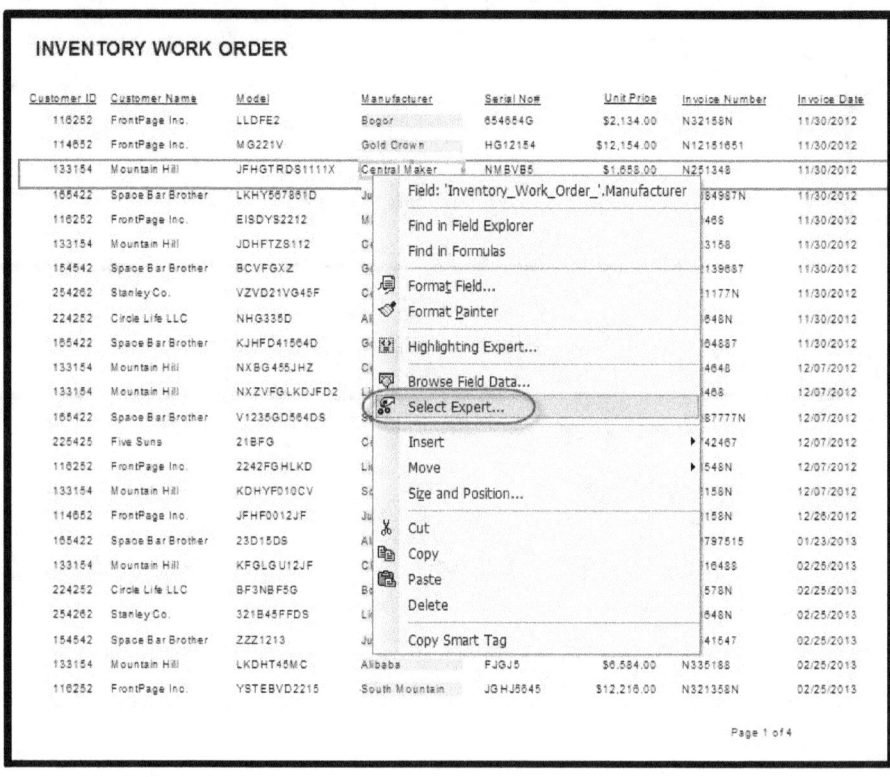

Figure 3.19 – *Right click on one of the objects in Manufacturer's field and choose Select Expert.*

Chapter 3 – FORMATTING A REPORT

Select Expert window appears, as shown below in figure 3.20.

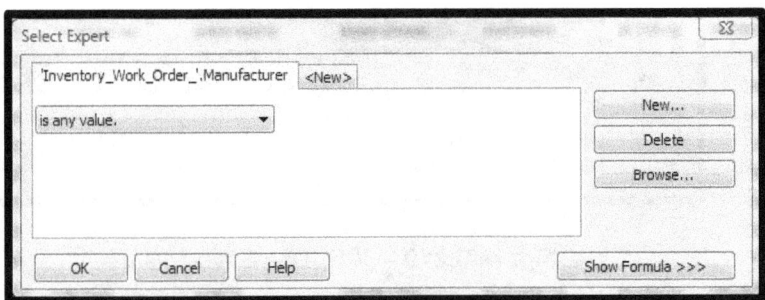

Figure 3.20 – Select Expert window

Let's filter the report and set where the **Manufacturer** value is equal to **Bogor** only. Click the first drop down menu and select "**Is equal to**" then click the second drop down menu and select "**Bogor**" and click **OK**, as shown below in figure 3.21a and 3.21b.

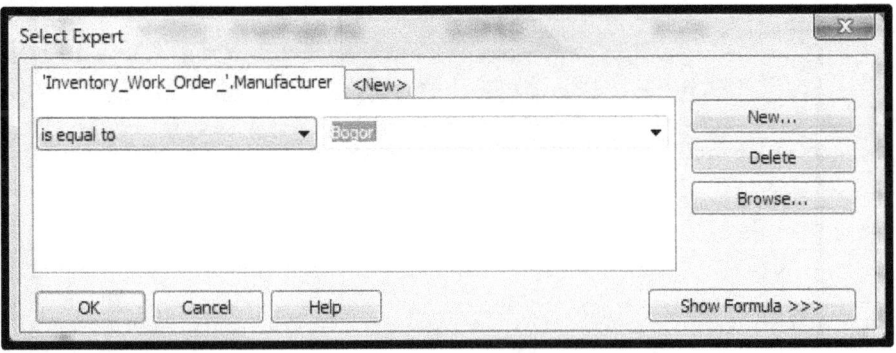

Figure 3.21a –Filter the Manufacturer value is equal to Bogor

Chapter 3 – FORMATTING A REPORT

Click "**Use Saved Data**", as shown below in figure *3.21b*.

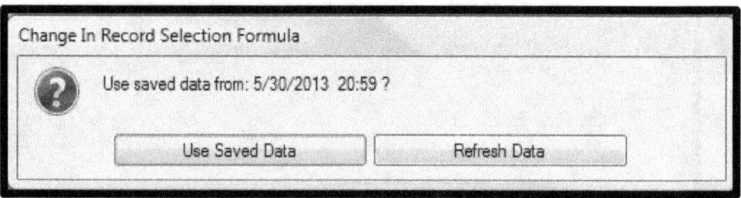

Figure 3.21b –Click "Use Saved Data"

The report now is showing only Manufacturers in "**Bogor**", as shown below in figure *3.21c*.

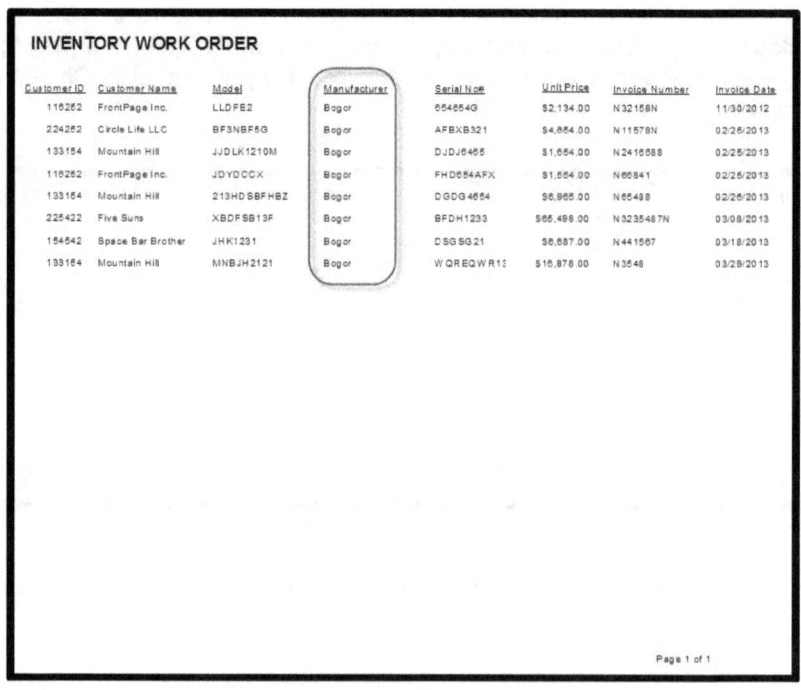

Figure 3.21c – *The report now shows Manufacturer Inventory Work Order in Bogor only.*

Chapter 3 – FORMATTING A REPORT

That narrowed the list a bit. Let's try another example. Suppose we want to see all records with a Unit Price between $1000 and $4000. Again, right click on one of the objects, this time in the Unit Price field, and choose **Select Expert**, as shown below in figure 3.22a.

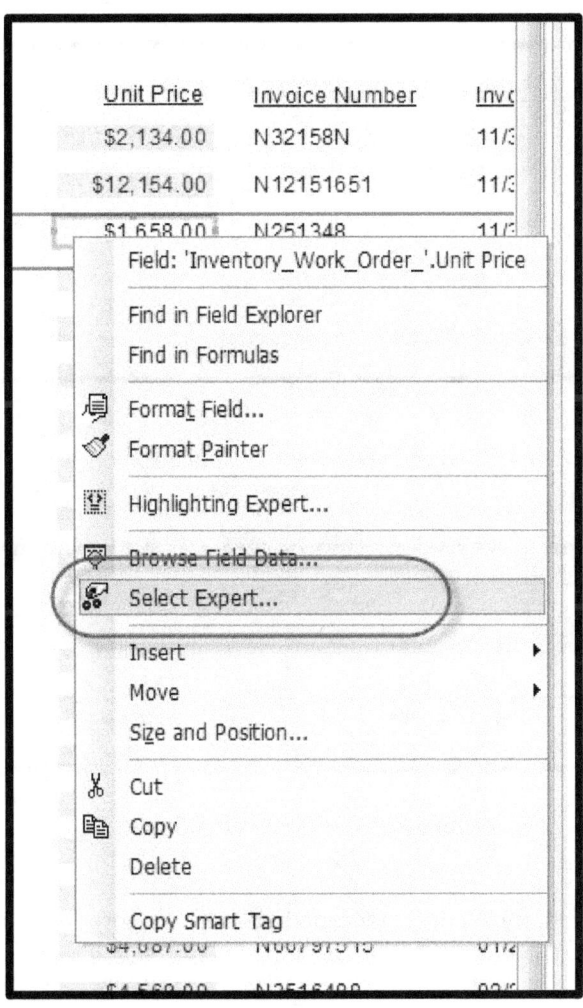

Figure 3.22a *– Right click on one of the objects in the Unit Price field and choose Select Expert.*

Chapter 3 – FORMATTING A REPORT

Now, in the left drop down menu, select "**Is Between**", and then in the other 2 drop down boxes enter $1000 and $4000. Click **OK**. When the pop-up menu asks if you wish to **Use Saved Data**, click **OK**, as shown below in figure *3.22b & 3.22c*.

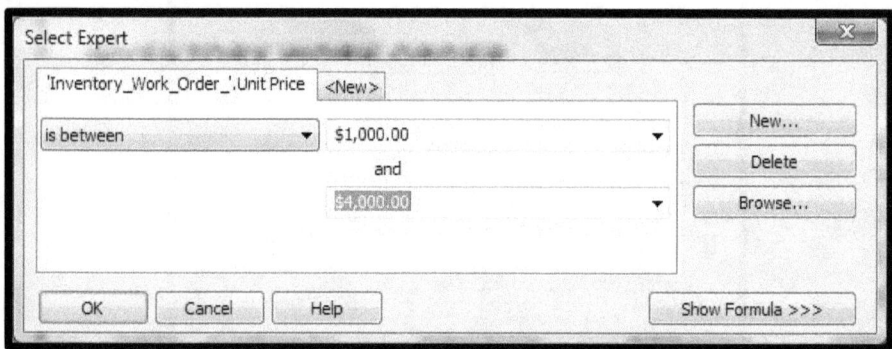

Figure 3.22b – *Choose In Between in Select Expert and place the price range*

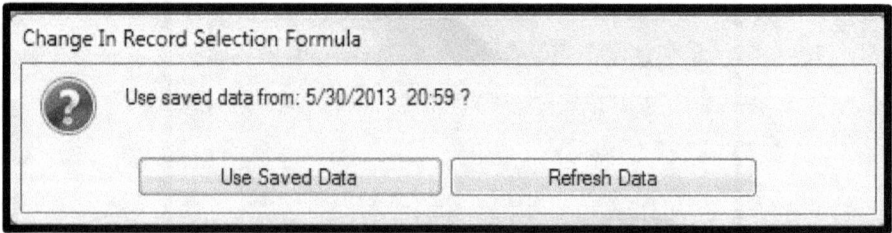

Figure 3.22c – *Click "Use Saved Data"*

The Inventory Work Order report now shows only the items with a Unit Price between $1,000 and $4,000, *as shown below in figure 3.22d.*

Chapter 3 – FORMATTING A REPORT

INVENTORY WORK ORDER

Customer ID	Customer Name	Model	Manufacturer	Serial No#	Unit Price	Invoice Number	Invoice Date
116262	FrontPage Inc.	LLDFE2	Bogor	654654G	$2,134.00	N32158N	11/30/2012
133154	Mountain Hill	JFHGTRDS1111X	Central Maker	NMBVB5	$1,658.00	N251348	11/30/2012
116252	FrontPage Inc.	EISDYS2212	Million Choice	DGDG4654	$1,235.00	N55468	11/30/2012
254262	Stanley Co.	VZVD21VG45F	Central Park	SDETGDS3	$1,354.00	N321177N	11/30/2012
165422	Space Bar Brother	KJHFD41564D	Gold Crown	DFH3213FJ	$1,879.00	N4664887	11/30/2012
133154	Mountain Hill	NXZVFGLKDJFD2	Lion King	WQE54	$3,564.00	N35468	12/07/2012
133154	Mountain Hill	KDHYF010CV	South Mountain	FGH654	$1,564.00	N32158N	12/07/2012
114652	FrontPage Inc.	JFHF0012JF	Jugle boy	HG546	$1,125.00	N13158N	12/26/2012
254262	Stanley Co.	321B45FFDS	Lion King	JF2TUYF	$1,265.00	N23648N	02/25/2013
133154	Mountain Hill	JJDLK1210M	Bogor	DJDJ6465	$1,654.00	N2416588	02/25/2013
116262	FrontPage Inc.	JDYDCCX	Bogor	FHD654AFX	$1,554.00	N66841	02/25/2013
133154	Mountain Hill	3546KMHBF	Central Park	MVBM21	$1,658.00	N3536	02/27/2013
254262	Stanley Co.	3CX21BFGFC321F	South Mountain	FGJDG324SG	$1,658.00	NN31NN	02/28/2013
133154	Mountain Hill	321JHFD	Jugle boy	BMFGJ1321	$1,687.00	N6648	02/28/2013
116262	FrontPage Inc.	KDHY457YTSA0	Gold Crown	XCB54	$1,526.00	N1547887	03/29/2013
114652	FrontPage Inc.	KLG0B	Center Plaza	HGG564	$1,515.00	N236858NN	03/29/2013
116262	FrontPage Inc.	LKDJHYTF445Z	South Mountain	FSE54	$1,564.00	N3534678N	03/29/2013
114652	FrontPage Inc.	RWYTS5424VV2	Central Park	GHG54	$1,215.00	N3213548	03/29/2013
254262	Stanley Co.	321DSG35VG	Chandler Side	FGJFYTSTSA	$1,687.00	NN15487NN	03/29/2013
116252	FrontPage Inc.	NCHDKY452GD	Center Plaza	FF45	$1,656.00	N331458	03/29/2013

Page 1 of 1

***Figure 3.22d** – The Inventory Work Order report now lists all records with a Unit Price between $1,000 and $4,000*

As mentioned before, **Crystal Reports** let you write your own filtering formulas, which adds a lot of flexibility and power to your output. It may seem confusing at first, but with just a little practice, you'll soon be writing code just like a pro. Let's give it a try. Right click on a field in the "**Customer Name**" column, and then choose **Select Expert**, as shown below in figure *3.23a*.

Chapter 3 – FORMATTING A REPORT

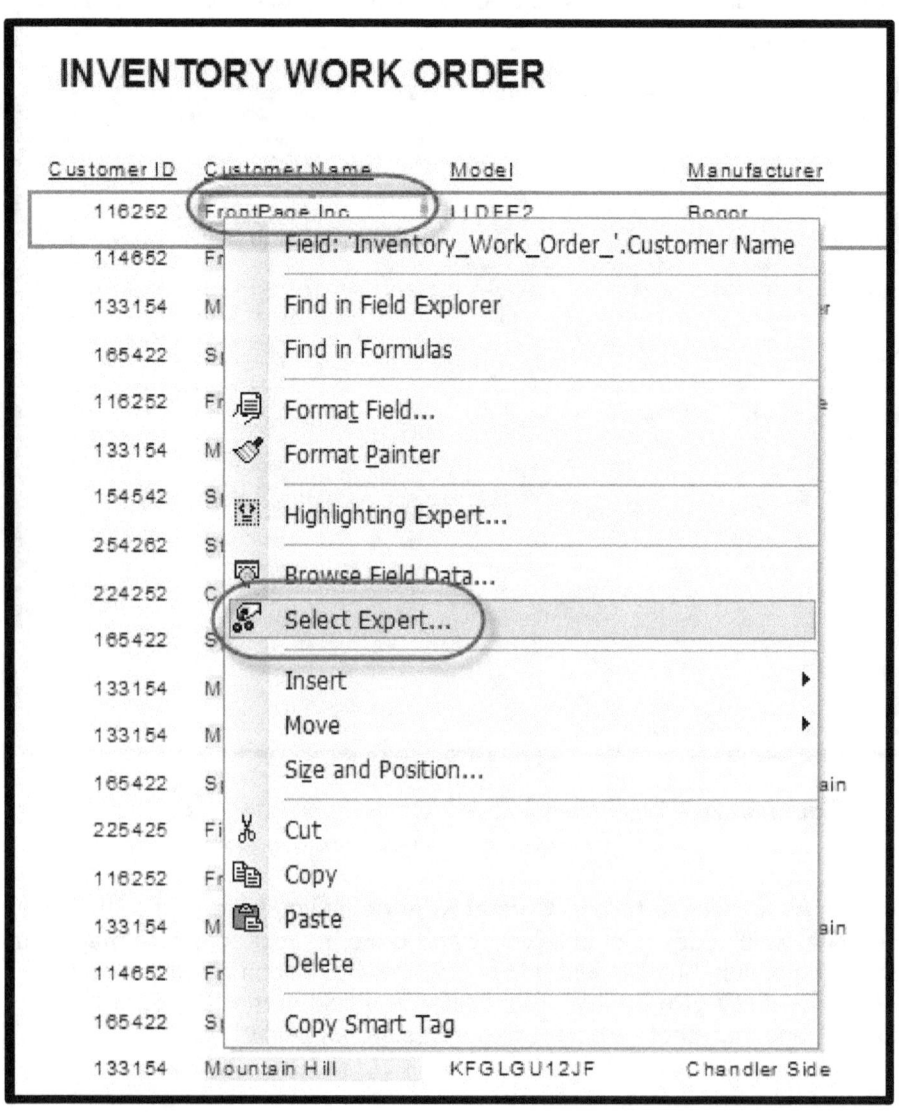

Figure 3.23a - Right click on one of the Customer Name fields

Chapter 3 – FORMATTING A REPORT

If you've ever written computer code before, you'll know how important it is to get the syntax exactly right. For this, **Select Editor** has a handy tool called the **Formula Editor**. To use the Editor, click the button labeled "**Show Formula**" on the right side of the Select Expert window, then click "**Formula Editor**", as shown below in figure 3.23b.

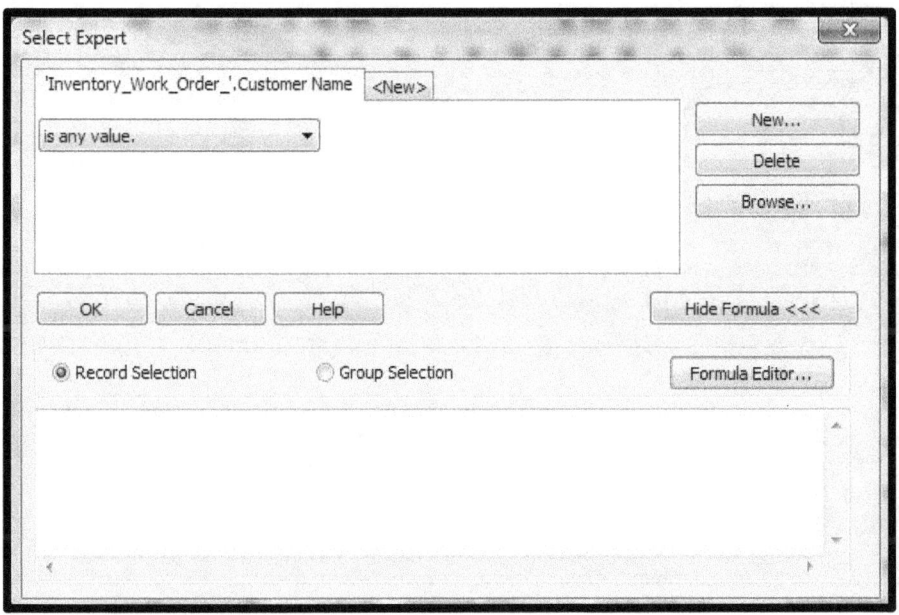

Figure 3.23b – Click "Show Formula" and "Formula Editor"

Chapter 3 – FORMATTING A REPORT

When you open the **Formula Editor**, the **Formula Workshop** and the **Record Selecting Formula Editor** appear, as shown below in figure *3.23c*.

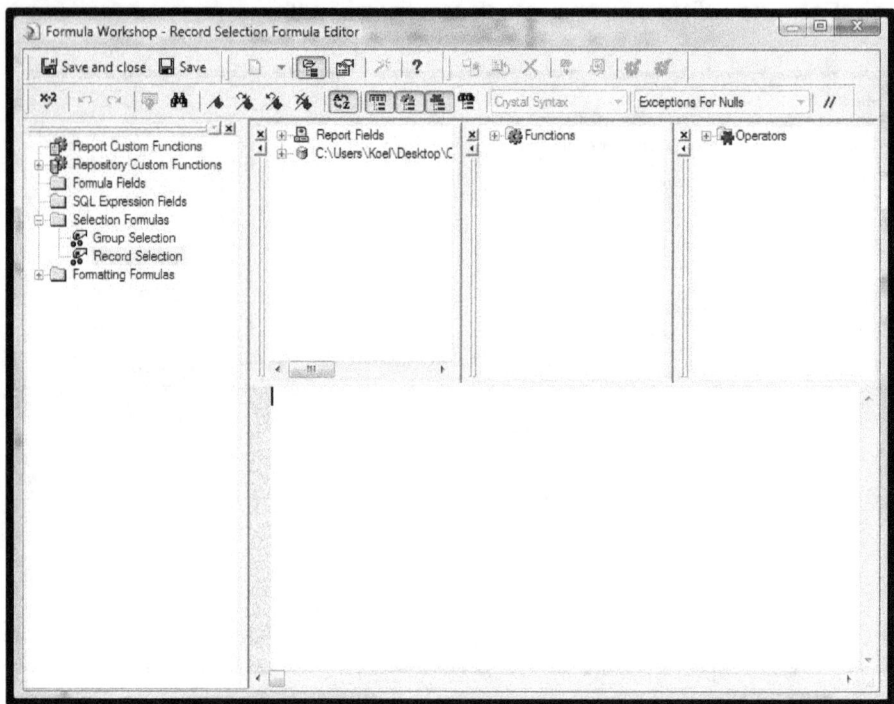

Figure 3.23c – *The Formula Workshop appears after you select the Formula Editor.*

Chapter 3 – FORMATTING A REPORT

Click the plus sign (**+**) to expand the **Report Fields** and double click on **Inventory Work Order Customer Name**, as shown below in figure 3.23d.

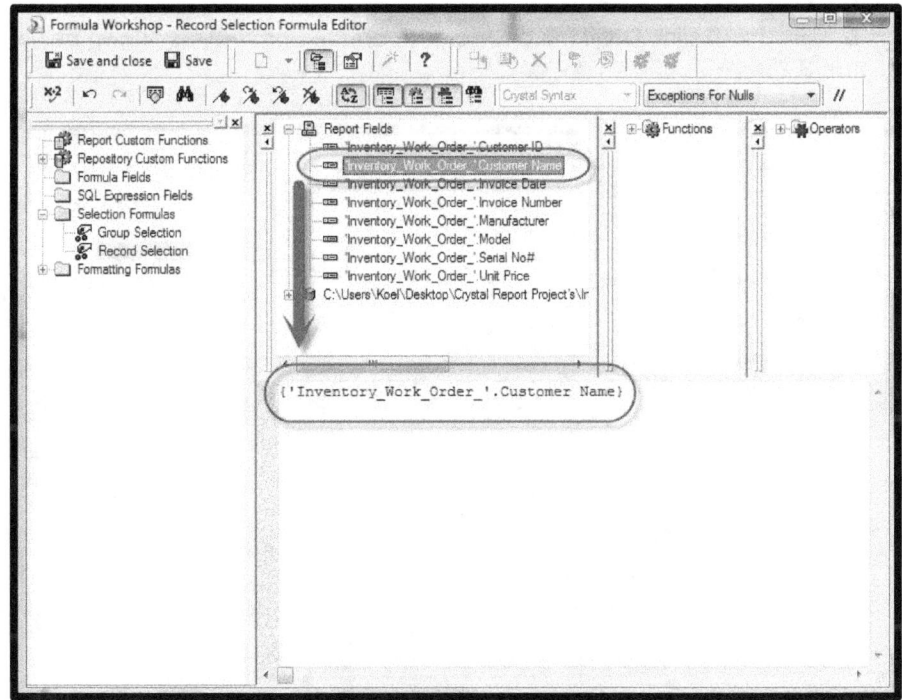

Figure 3.23d – click the plus sign (+) to expand the Report Fields

Type the equal sign (**=**), opening double quotation (**"**), *FrontPage Inc.*, and closing double quotation (**"**) , as shown below in figure 3.23e.

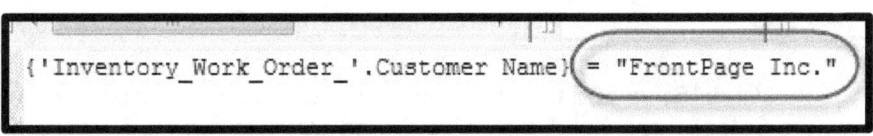

Figure 3.23e – Type = "FrontPage Inc."

Chapter 3 – FORMATTING A REPORT

To check whether or not the formula has an error, click the **X+2** check sign and click **OK** if there is no error on the Formula, as shown below in figure 3.23f.

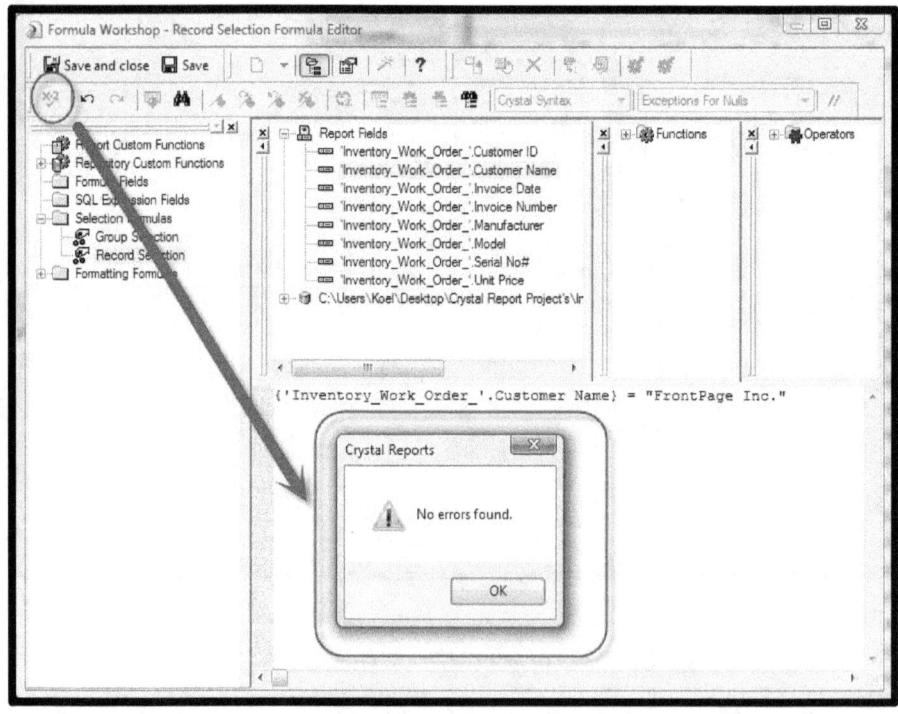

Figure 3.23f – click the X+2 check icon to check if the Formula has an error or not

Click "**Save and Close**" to close the Formula Workshop then click **OK** on the **Select Expert** and click "**Use Saved Data**" to run the Formula on the report, as shown below in figure 3.23g, 3.23h, and 3.23i.

Chapter 3 – FORMATTING A REPORT

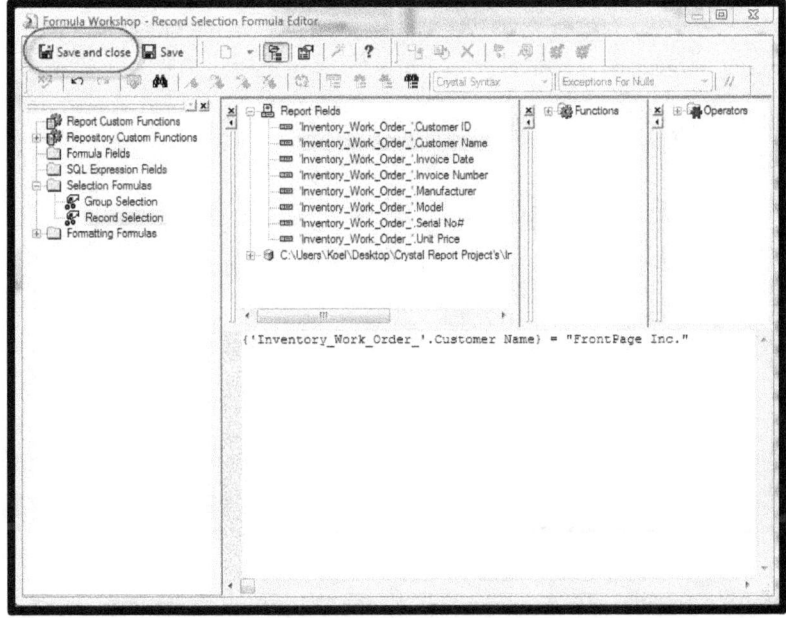

Figure 3.23g - Click Save and Close to close the Formula Workshop.

Chapter 3 – FORMATTING A REPORT

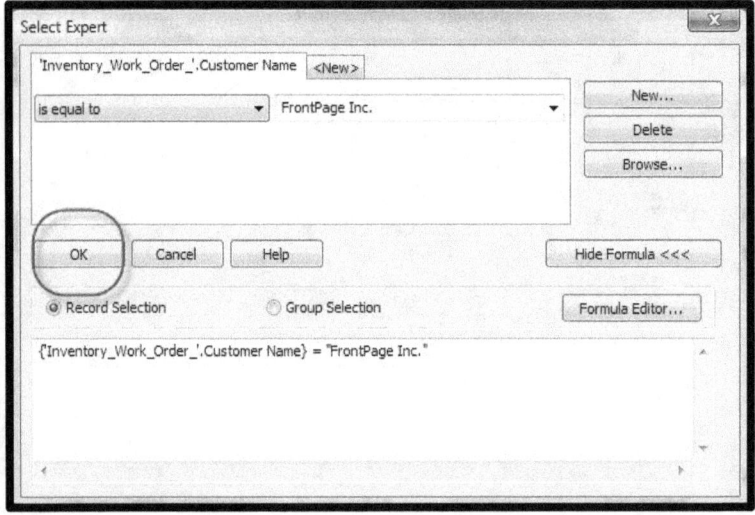

Figure 3.23h – Click OK on the Select Expert to run the Formula on the Report

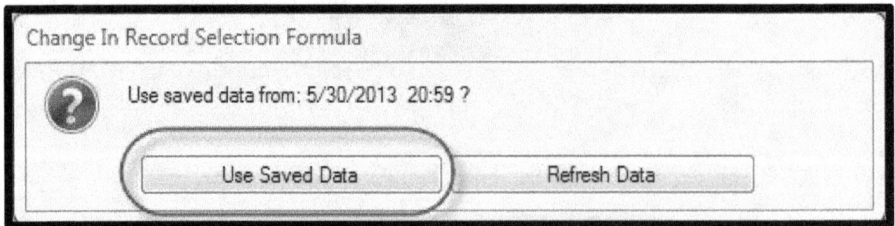

Figure 3.23i – Click Use Saved Data

The Inventory Work Order Report has now been filtered to show only **FrontPage Inc**. in the **Customer Name** column, as shown below in figure *3.23j*.

Chapter 3 – FORMATTING A REPORT

INVENTORY WORK ORDER

Customer ID	Customer Name	Model	Manufacturer	Serial No#	Unit Price	Invoice Number	Invoice Date
116252	FrontPage Inc.	LLDFE2	Bogor	654654G	$2,134.00	N32158N	11/30/2012
114652	FrontPage Inc.	MG221V	Gold Crown	HG12154	$12,154.00	N12151651	11/30/2012
116252	FrontPage Inc.	EISDYS2212	Million Choice	DGDG4654	$1,236.00	N55468	11/30/2012
116252	FrontPage Inc.	2242FGHLKD	Lion King	GDG45	$4,648.00	N33548N	12/07/2012
114652	FrontPage Inc.	JFHF0012JF	Jugle boy	HG546	$1,125.00	N13158N	12/26/2012
116252	FrontPage Inc.	YSTEBVD2215	South Mountain	JGHJ5645	$12,216.00	N321358N	02/26/2013
114652	FrontPage Inc.	LGKJ012UY	Malay Man	HG45646	$21,354.00	N65438N	02/25/2013
116252	FrontPage Inc.	GCFDT2312	Chandler Side	RR6454RY	$5,465.00	N548574	02/25/2013
116252	FrontPage Inc.	00HFT0	Alibaba	FHF465	$16,578.00	N55677	02/25/2013
116252	FrontPage Inc.	JDYDCCX	Bogor	FHD654AFX	$1,554.00	N66841	02/25/2013
114652	FrontPage Inc.	KLGKF5554	Central Maker	HG54645	$21,213.00	N13248	02/26/2013
116252	FrontPage Inc.	MCXBCG5455	Central Park	XB654564B	$21,668.00	N55687	02/26/2013
116252	FrontPage Inc.	NXV2245GDH	Jugle boy	XCBB654	$13,654.00	N33548N	03/29/2013
116252	FrontPage Inc.	KDHY457YTSA0	Gold Crown	XCB54	$1,526.00	N1547887	03/29/2013
114652	FrontPage Inc.	KLG0B	Center Plaza	HGG564	$1,515.00	N236858NN	03/29/2013
116252	FrontPage Inc.	LKDJHYTF445Z	South Mountain	FSE54	$1,564.00	N3534678N	03/29/2013
116252	FrontPage Inc.	DXSZ	Alibaba	FFF5A64	$5,468.00	N1135484	03/29/2013
114652	FrontPage Inc.	RWYTS5424VV2	Central Park	GHG54	$1,215.00	N3213548	03/29/2013
116252	FrontPage Inc.	NCHDKY452GD	Center Plaza	FF45	$1,656.00	N331458	03/29/2013

Page 1 of 1

Figure 3.23j *– Inventory Work Order report now shows only the FrontPage Inc. Customer Name*

Great! Now you know how to format your data using conditions and formulas in **Select Expert**.

Chapter 3 – FORMATTING A REPORT

Section Expert

The last formatting feature to be discussed is the **Section Expert**. In Chapter 2, I described the five default main sections in *Crystal Reports*. They are **Report Header**, **Page Header**, **Details**, **Report Footer** and **Page Footer**. The **Section Expert** is used to handle the formatting of one, or all, of the five main sections.

There two ways to activate the **Section Expert**:

1. Go to the Report drop down list on the menu bar, and click **Section Expert**, as show below in figure 3.24.

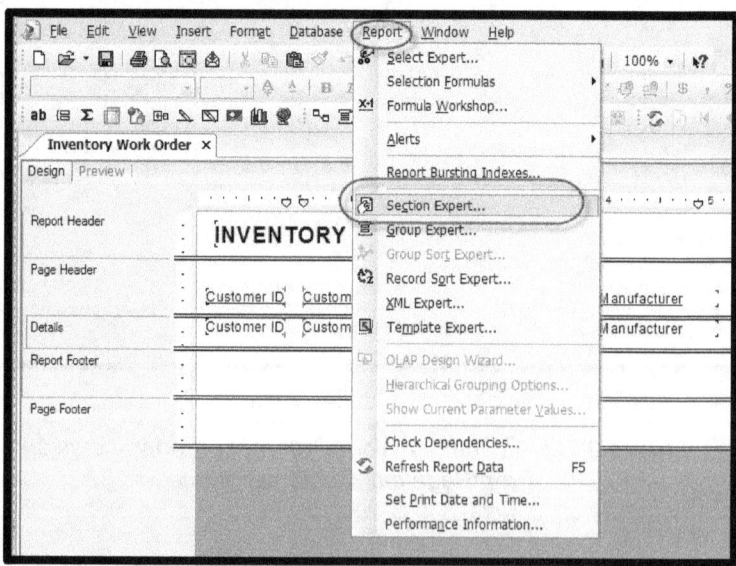

Figure 3.24 – *Go to Report on menu bar and select Section Expert*

Chapter 3 – FORMATTING A REPORT

2. Right click on either the **Design** or **Preview** tab in one of the report sections and select **Section Expert**., as shown below in figure *3.25a and 3.25b*.

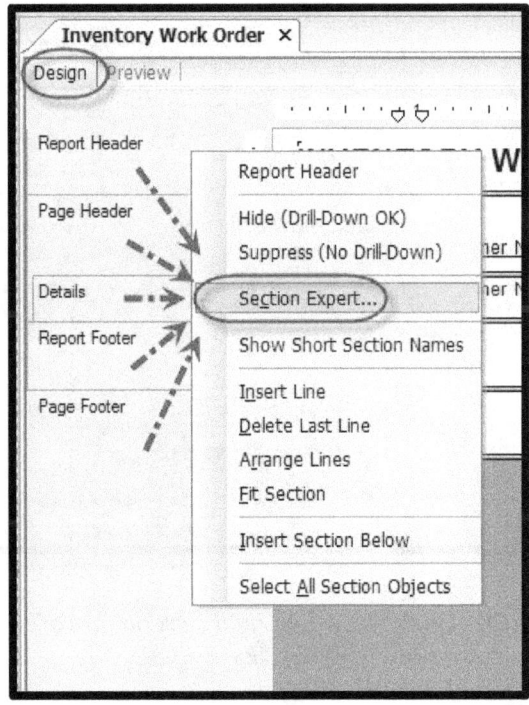

Figure 3.25a – *On Design tab, right click on one of sections and select Section Expert.*

Chapter 3 – FORMATTING A REPORT

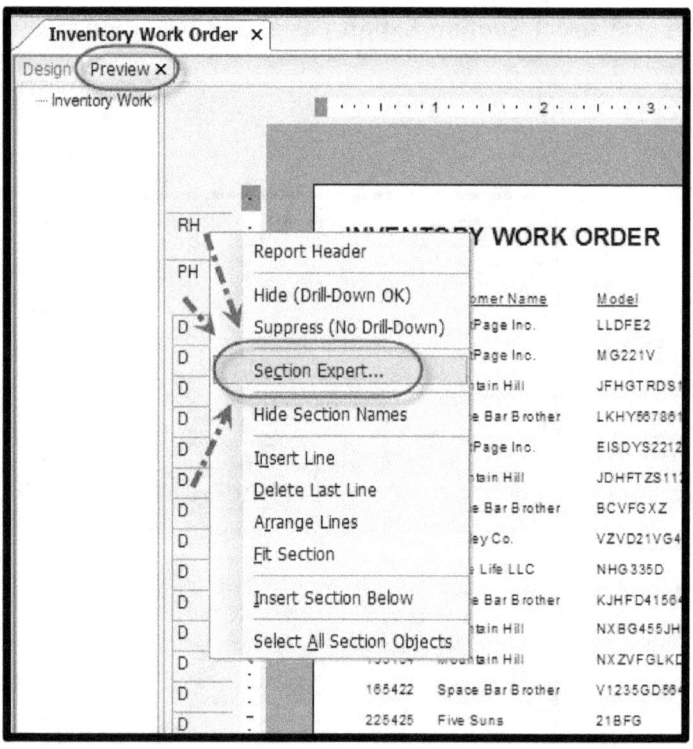

Figure 3.25b - On Preview tab, right click on one of sections and select Section Expert.

Chapter 3 – FORMATTING A REPORT

Let me explain to you what the **Sections**, **Common,** and **Color** tabs are in the **Section Expert**, as shown below in figure *3.26*.

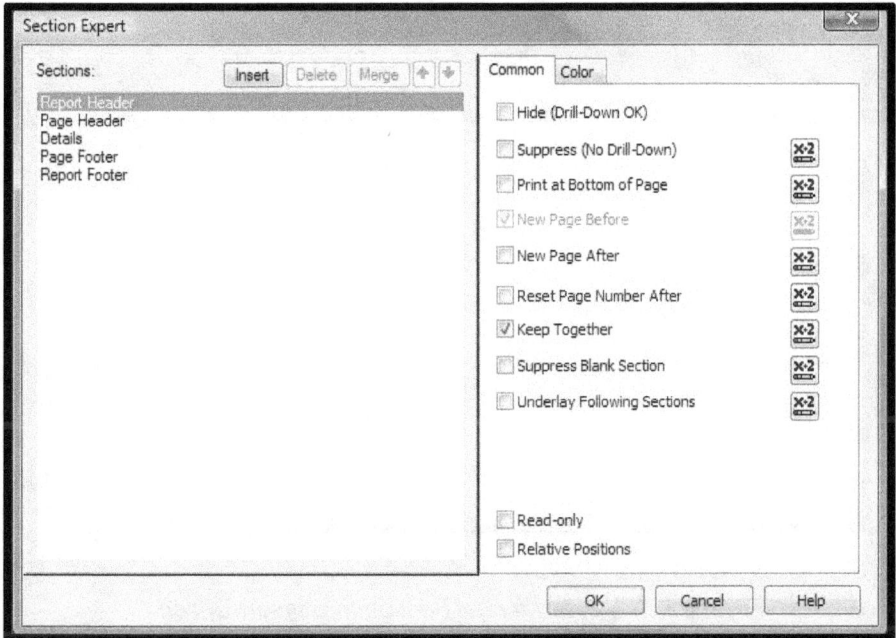

Figure 3.26 – *Section Expert*

Sections

- **Insert** – This option allows you to insert a new section of the same type as the section you have selected in the section list.

    Example: Choose the **Report Header** as your selected section and insert an additional **Report Header** by clicking **Insert**. You now have two **Report Headers**, **A** and **B**, as shown below in figure 3.27.

Chapter 3 – FORMATTING A REPORT

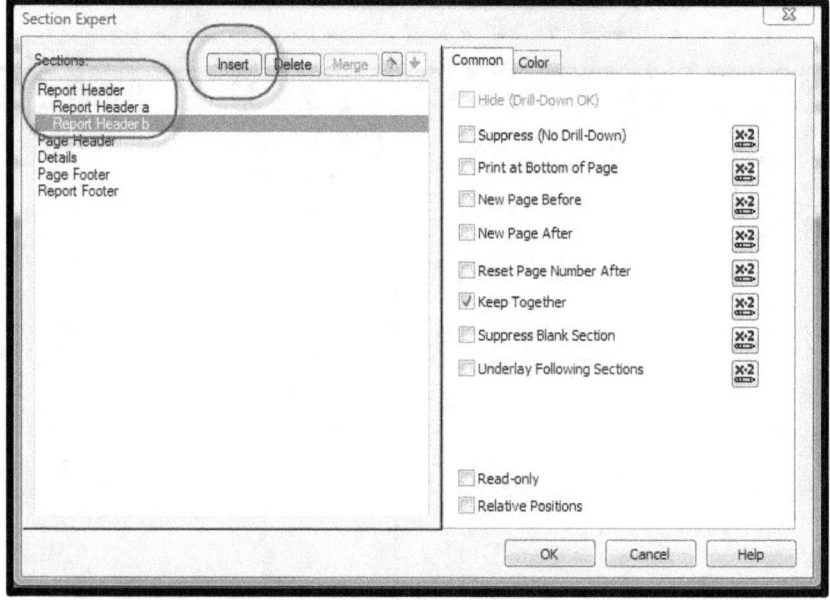

Figure 3.27 – *Insert a new Section thru Insert Option.*

- **Delete** – This option allows you to delete the section you have selected in the section list.

- **Merge** – This option will allow you to merge the current section with the section below it.

Based on the above example, you have two **Report Headers**, **A** and **B**. Select **Report Header A** and click **Merge**. Now, **A** and **B** are combined and the name changed back to **Report Header**, as shown below in figure *3.28a* and *3.28b*.

Chapter 3 – FORMATTING A REPORT

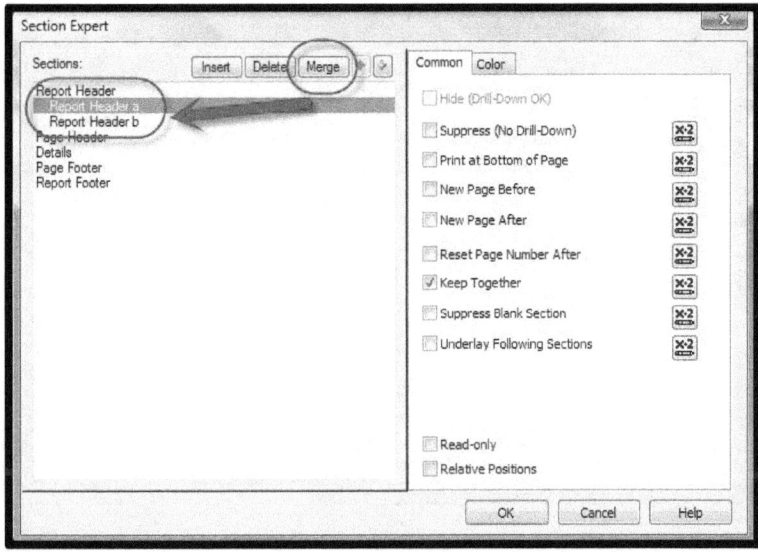

Figure 3.28a *– Select the top Report Header (A) and click Merge to merge the Report Headers*

Chapter 3 – FORMATTING A REPORT

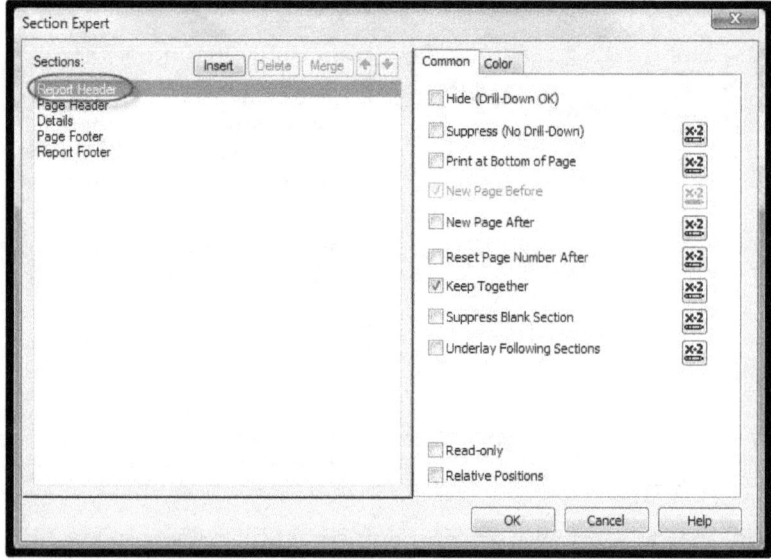

Figure 3.28b – *Report Header merged thru the Merge option*

- **Arrow buttons**– This option will allow you to move the related section up or down.

Common tab

- **Hide** (Drill-Down OK) – This option will hide sections you do not want to print but that you want to be available for drill-down (if included in the group of the Summary Report). When you hide the detail group section, you are able to display the **Details** section if you double click the group itself.

Chapter 3 – FORMATTING A REPORT

For example:

In the **Inventory Work Order**, I inserted a group by the **Customer Name**. Now, right click on the Details section, select **Section Expert,** and then choose **Hide**, as shown below in figure *3.29a, 3.29b, 3.29c and 3.29d*.

Figure 3.29a – Group by Customer Name

Reporting With Visual Crystal Reports

Chapter 3 – FORMATTING A REPORT

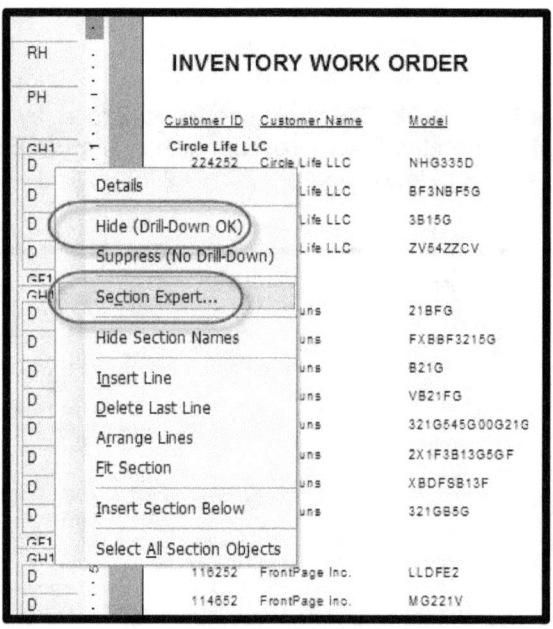

Figure 3.29b – *Choose Section Expert, or directly click Hide from the drop down menu to hide the Details section.*

Chapter 3 – FORMATTING A REPORT

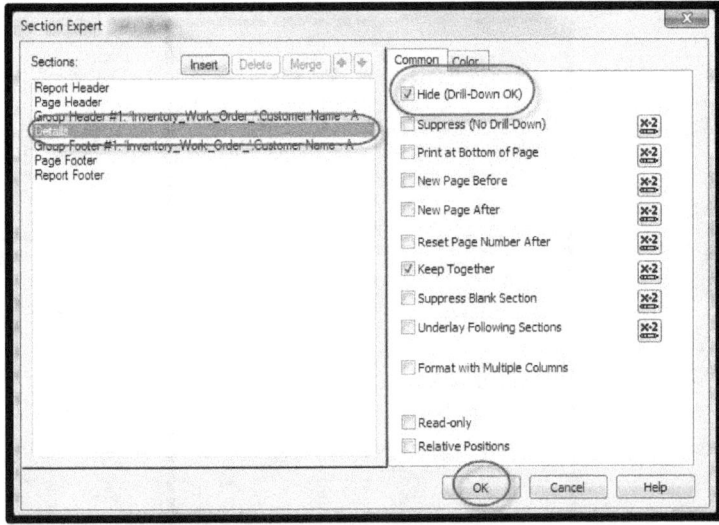

Figure 3.29c – *Make sure the Details section is selected then click Hide and OK to hide Details section*

All of the **Details** have now disappeared except the group name. Now, click on one of the group names, and the Details will appear by the group, as shown below in figure *3.29d and 3.29e*.

Chapter 3 – FORMATTING A REPORT

Figure 3.29d – *All the details on the report have disappeared except the group name.*

Five Suns								
225425	Five Suns	21BFG	Central Park	GJKHGK212	$4,588.00	N9742467	12/07/2012
225422	Five Suns	FXBBF3215G	Chandler Side	SDGXB21	$46,897.00	N213648	02/25/2013
225425	Five Suns	B21G	Jugle boy	GH131	$4,848.00	N1134588	02/25/2013
225422	Five Suns	VB21FG	Alibaba	DSDGG121	$898.00	N33558	02/25/2013
225425	Five Suns	321G545G00G21G	Lion King	FST2131	$46,548.00	N101348N	02/25/2013
225425	Five Suns	2X1F3B13G5GF	Central Maker	ETETST21	$4,675.00	NN32154NN	02/28/2013
225422	Five Suns	XBDFSB13F	Bogor	BFDH1233	$65,498.00	N3235487N	03/08/2013
225425	Five Suns	321GB5G	Center Plaza	DHDHK321	$545.00	N134187N	03/29/2013

Figure 3.29e – *You can still see the Report's Details by clicking to one of the Group names*

Chapter 3 – FORMATTING A REPORT

Note: Notice that in the Design Tab/view, the Details background changes when you hide the section, as shown below in figure 3.30.

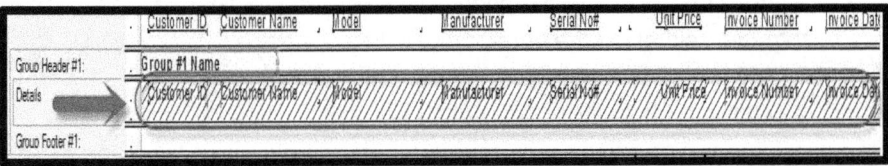

Figure 3.30 - Details background changes when you hide the section

Note: Drill-down means to move from summary information to detail data by focusing on something or to examine information at another level or in greater detail, especially in a database, to navigate to more detailed level or record.

- **Suppress** (No Drill-Down) – This option will hide the section you wish not to print and the content for drill-down as well. This is the opposite of the Hide option. You will not see the Report's detail when you click the group

- **Print at Bottom of Page** – This option will allow each group value to print only at the bottom of a page. This option is useful for printing invoices and other reports with a single group to appear on a page and the value for that group to print only at the bottom of the page.

- **New Page Before**–This option will set a page break before it prints the section for group (the Header and Footer) and details.

Chapter 3 – FORMATTING A REPORT

- **New Page After**–This option will set a page break after it prints the section for group (the Header and Footer) and details

- **Reset Page Number After** – This option will allow you to reset the page number to one (1) for the following page, after it prints a group total.

- **Keep Together** –This option will keep all the lines of the section together, either on the current or on the next page.

> **Note:** *This option does not apply to multi-line string or memo field. A page break may apply in the middle of a multi-line field.*

- **Suppress Blank Section** – This option will hide the section if it is blank, and prints it if it is not.

- **Underlay Following Section** – This option will underlay the following section(s) when it prints.

- **Read-only** – This option will disable all the formatting in all the sections.

- **Relative Positions** – This option will allow you to lock an object in its original position on the report.

Color

Background Color – This option will allow you to set the background color of the section.

Chapter 4 – GROUPING, SUMMARY AND RUNNING TOTAL

Grouping Data

Grouping in Crystal Reports is an easy way to sort, subtotal, arrange, and perform other useful operations with your data. Some of the benefits of grouping data in a report are to make it look organized, easy to view, and easy to read. In Crystal Reports, you have two ways to access the grouping feature. First, you can click Report on the menu bar and choose **Group Expert**, or you can click on the Insert dropdown and find **Insert Group**, as shown below in figure 4.0a & 4.0b.

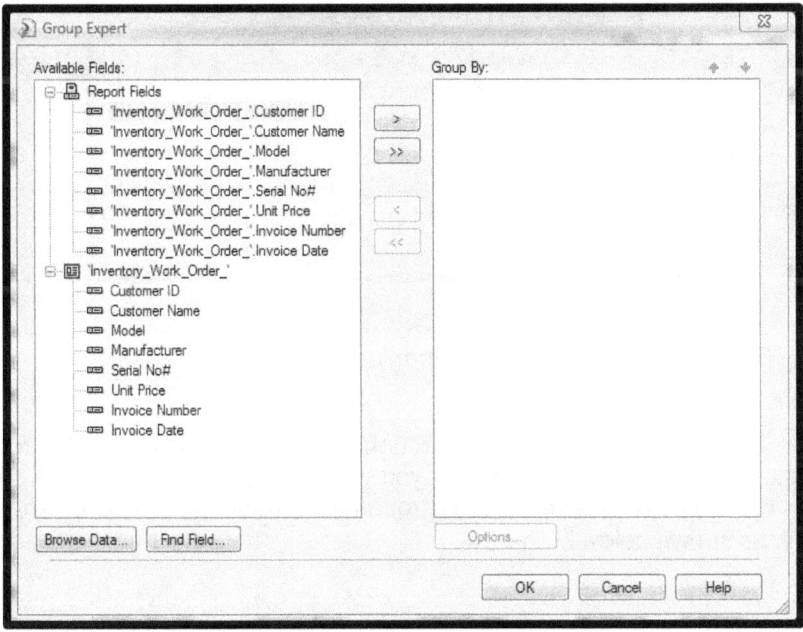

Figure 4.0a – *Group Expert, from Report dropdown on Menu bar.*

Chapter 4 – GROUPING, SUMMARY AND RUNNING TOTAL

Figure 4.0b – Insert Group, from Insert dropdown on Menu bar.

Selecting a field of records through **Insert Group** will allow you to sort the data for that group. However, if you use **Group Expert**, you can select one or more groups of records, and group all of them **by** the field criteria you specify, as shown below in figure 4.1.

Chapter 4 – GROUPING, SUMMARY AND RUNNING TOTAL

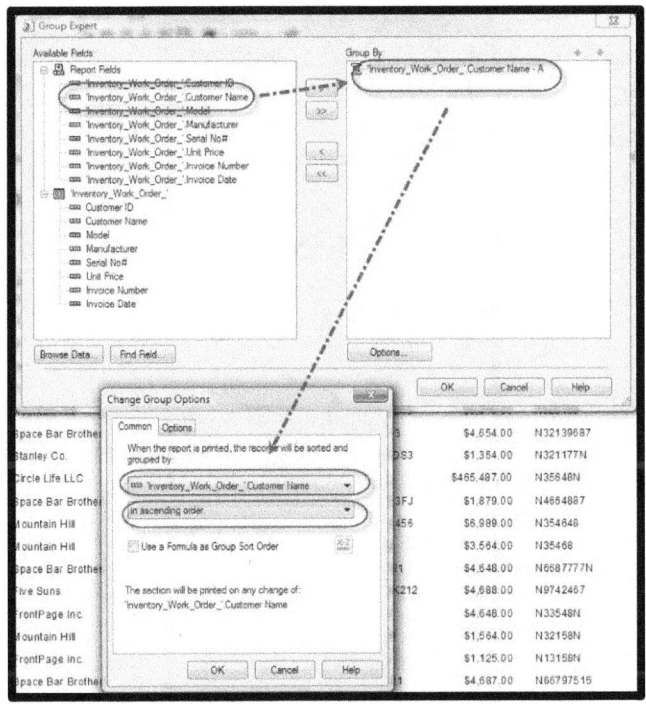

Figure 4.1 – *Once you have selected the field(s) for grouping, Crystal Reports will allow you to sort the data.*

Insert Group

In this grouping example, you will see how to group the **Inventory Work Order** report by the **Customer Name**. Click on **Insert**, **Group,** select **Group by Customer Name**, and click **OK**, as shown below in figure 4.2a and 4.2b.

Chapter 4 – GROUPING, SUMMARY AND RUNNING TOTAL

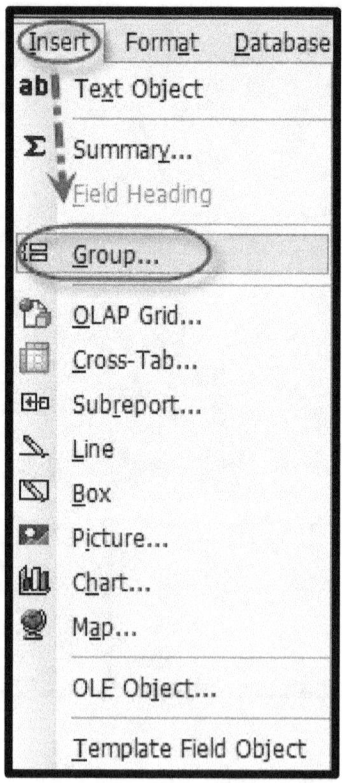

Figure 4.2a – *Go to Insert, Group.*

Chapter 4 – GROUPING, SUMMARY AND RUNNING TOTAL

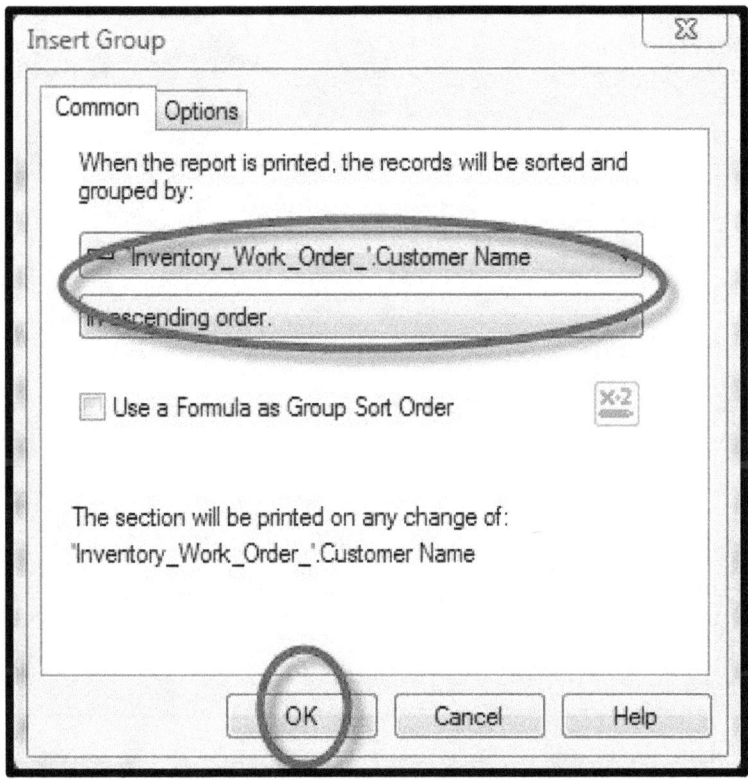

Figure 4.2b – Select Group by Customer Name.

Now the Inventory Work Order report has been ordered into groups of sales by Customer Name in ascending alphabetical order, as shown below in figure 4.3.

Chapter 4 – GROUPING, SUMMARY AND RUNNING TOTAL

INVENTORY WORK ORDER							
Customer ID	Customer Name	Model	Manufacturer	Serial No#	Unit Price	Invoice Number	Invoice Date
Circle Life LLC							
224252	Circle Life LLC	NHG335D	Alibaba	AZSF21	$465,487.00	N35648N	11/30/2012
224252	Circle Life LLC	BF3NBF5G	Bogor	AFBXB321	$4,654.00	N11578N	02/26/2013
224252	Circle Life LLC	3B15G	Central Park	GSDGST1	$689.00	NN16548	02/28/2013
224252	Circle Life LLC	ZV54ZZCV	Jugle boy	SDGSDG21	$46,897.00	N3321574N	03/29/2013
Five Suns							
225425	Five Suns	21BFG	Central Park	GJKHGK212	$4,688.00	N9742467	12/07/2012
225422	Five Suns	FXBBF3215G	Chandler Side	SDGXB21	$46,897.00	N213648	02/26/2013
225425	Five Suns	B21G	Jugle boy	GH131	$4,648.00	N1134588	02/26/2013
225422	Five Suns	VB21FG	Alibaba	DSDGG121	$898.00	N33558	02/26/2013
225425	Five Suns	321G546G00G21G	Lion King	FST2131	$46,548.00	N101348N	02/26/2013
225425	Five Suns	2X1F3B13G5GF	Central Maker	ETETST21	$4,675.00	NN32154NN	02/28/2013
225422	Five Suns	XBDFSB13F	Bogor	BFDH1233	$65,498.00	N3235487N	03/08/2013
225425	Five Suns	321GB5G	Center Plaza	DHDHK321	$645.00	N134187N	03/29/2013
FrontPage Inc.							
116252	FrontPage Inc.	LLDFE2	Bogor	654654G	$2,134.00	N32158N	11/30/2012
114652	FrontPage Inc.	MG221V	Gold Crown	HG12154	$12,154.00	N12151551	11/30/2012
116252	FrontPage Inc.	EISDYS2212	Million Choice	DGDG4554	$1,235.00	N55468	11/30/2012
116252	FrontPage Inc.	2242FGHLKD	Lion King	GDG45	$4,648.00	N33548N	12/07/2012
114652	FrontPage Inc.	JFHF0012JF	Jugle boy	HG546	$1,125.00	N13158N	12/26/2012
116252	FrontPage Inc.	YSTEBVD2215	South Mountain	JGHJ5645	$12,216.00	N321358N	02/26/2013
114652	FrontPage Inc.	LGKJ012UY	Malay Man	HG45646	$21,354.00	N55438N	02/26/2013

Page 1 of 4

Figure 4.3 – The Inventory Work Order report is grouped by Customer Name in ascending order.

Chapter 4 – GROUPING, SUMMARY AND RUNNING TOTAL

Group Expert

Now, suppose you wish to also arrange the Customer Name groups by **Manufacturer**. Repeat the same steps as before; using Group Expert, but this time, select **Manufacturer** as the field to Group By.

To do this, first select the Group Expert option from the Report tab on the menu bar. Next, select **Manufacturer** from the **available field** choices on the left side of the "**Group By"** window, and use the right arrow key (looks like a "greater than" symbol) to move it over to the right side. Finally, click the **Options** button and select **Ascending Order**. See examples, as shown below in figure 4.4a, 4.4b, & 4.4c.

Chapter 4 – GROUPING, SUMMARY AND RUNNING TOTAL

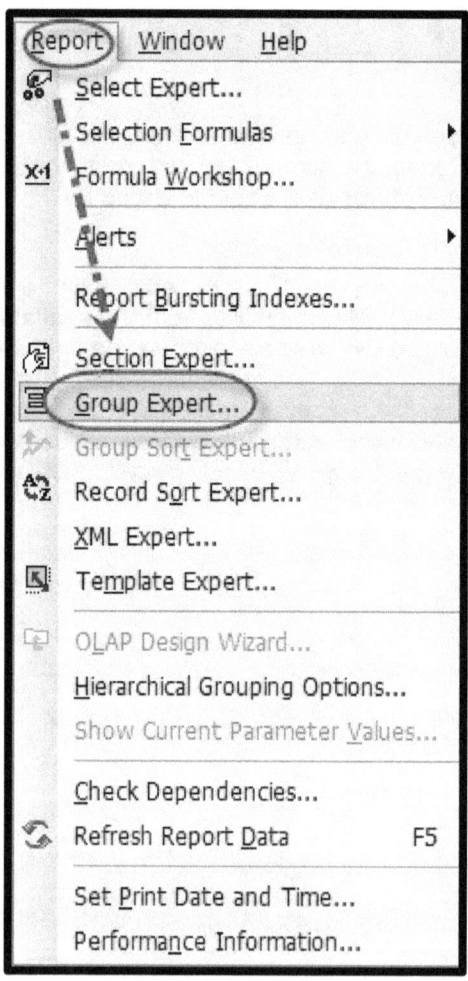

Figure 4.4a - From the Report menu tab, chooses Group Expert.

Chapter 4 – GROUPING, SUMMARY AND RUNNING TOTAL

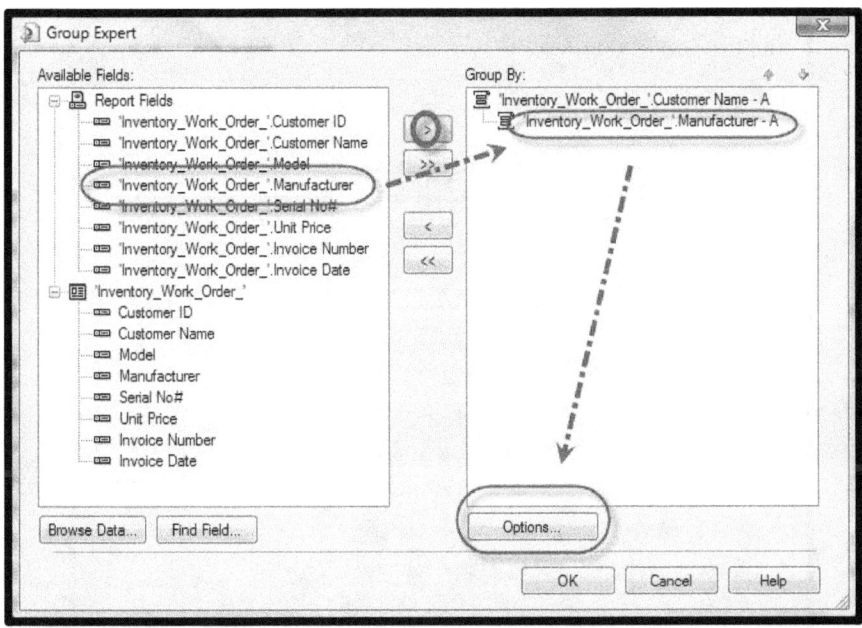

Figure 4.4b – Select "'Inventory_Work_Order_'.Manufacturer" from the window on the left, use the right arrow key to move the field to the right, and then click **Options**.

Chapter 4 – GROUPING, SUMMARY AND RUNNING TOTAL

Figure 4.4c – *Sort the Manufacturer groups in ascending order.*

The **Inventory Work Order** report now has two header groupings (see **GH1** and **GH2**, as shown below in figure 4.5). For clarity, I've indented group header 2 slightly to indicate that it is a subset of group 1.

Chapter 4 – GROUPING, SUMMARY AND RUNNING TOTAL

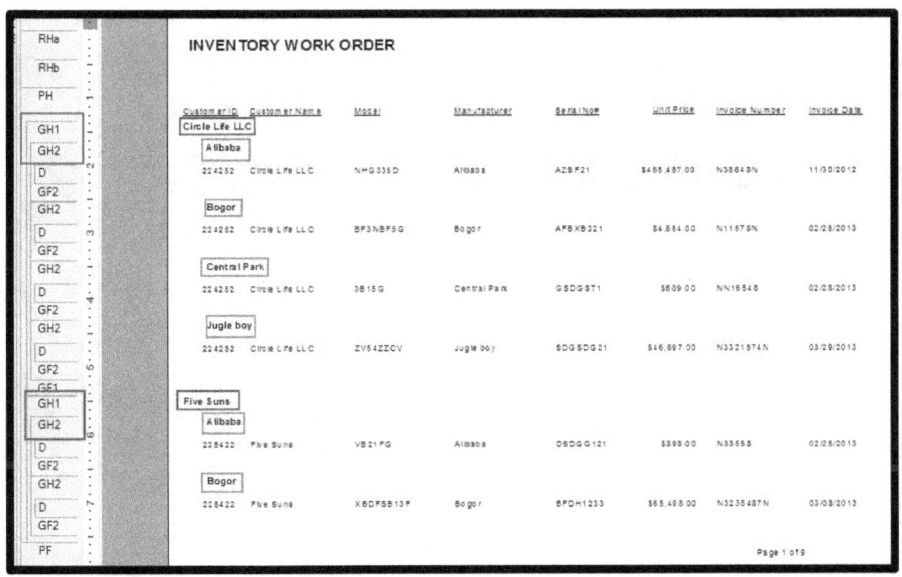

Figure 4.5 – *Inventory Work Order report now has two groups, GH1 and GH2.*

As discussed in chapter 3, Crystal Reports has a tool called Section Expert which is used for modifying and customizing section properties. In the **Section Expert**, you will see the name of each field that is being used for grouping and sorting. Go to "**Report**" on the menu bar and choose **Section Expert**. Notice that each section has its own Group Header and Group Footer, as shown below in figure 4.6.

The Group Footer is the area where group data is summed and summarized. The "Summary" function is used for this purpose [**Σ Summary...**]. We will take a closer look at this subject later in this chapter.

Chapter 4 – GROUPING, SUMMARY AND RUNNING TOTAL

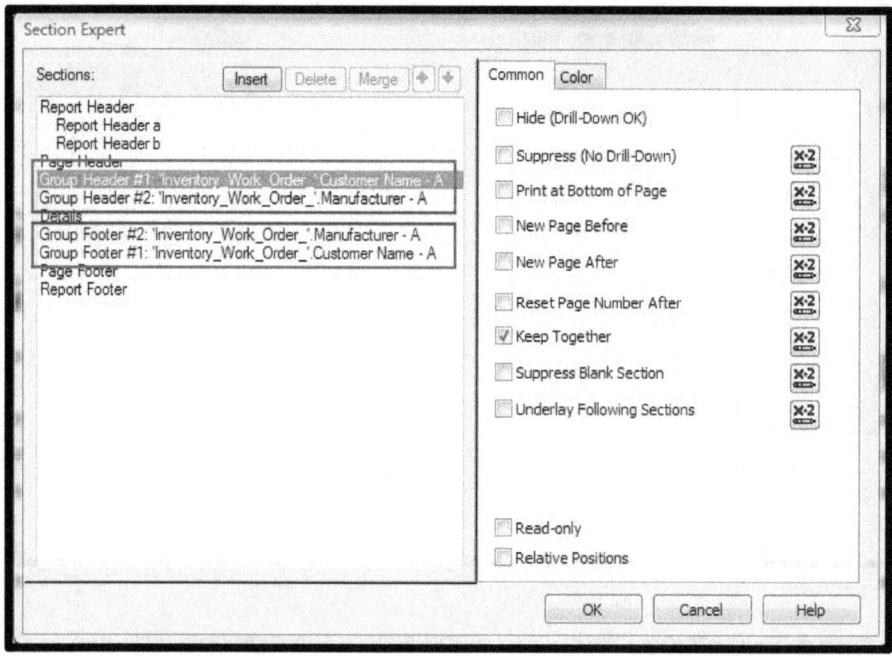

Figure 4.6 – *In Section Expert you can see the field name of each group.*

Group Sort Expert

The **Group Sort Expert** allows you to sort and identify the top or bottom group so the report will display only the range of items you wish to see. For example, in the group **Circle Life LL**, suppose you only need to see the Top 2 entries out of a total of 4 Manufacturers listed. **Assuming the report is summarized**, you can use the Summary feature to "**filter**" the list. Figures 4.7a and 4.7b shows the report output before filtering.

Chapter 4 – GROUPING, SUMMARY AND RUNNING TOTAL

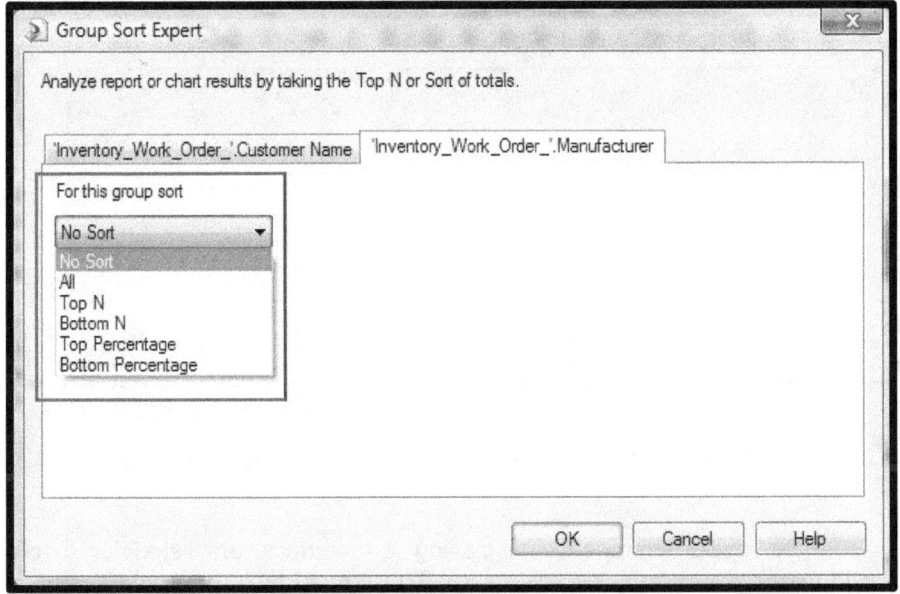

Figure 4.7a – Group Sort Expert dialog and sort lists.

Chapter 4 – GROUPING, SUMMARY AND RUNNING TOTAL

Customer ID	Customer Name	Model	Manufacturer	Serial No#	Unit Price	Invoice Number	Invoice Date
Circle Life LLC							
Alibaba							
224252	Circle Life LLC	NHG335D	Alibaba	AZSF21	$465,487.00	N35648N	11/30/2012
Bogor							
224252	Circle Life LLC	BF3NBF5G	Bogor	AFBXB321	$4,654.00	N11578N	02/25/2013
Central Park							
224252	Circle Life LLC	3B15G	Central Park	GSDGST1	$689.00	NN16548	02/28/2013
Jugle boy							
224252	Circle Life LLC	ZV54ZZCV	Jugle boy	SDGSDG21	$46,897.00	N3321574N	03/29/2013

Figure 4.7b – Group in Circle Life LLC has four manufacturers.

The report is presently displaying 4 manufacturers listed for **Circle Life LLC**. To show only records for the Top 2 manufacturers (by unit price), go to the menu bar, select **Record** and **Group Sort Expert**. Choose sort **Top N** and enter the number **2** where prompted. Click **OK** to see the filtered results, as shown below in figure 4.7c, 4.7d, & 4.7e.

Note: *Make sure you select the correct group tab in the Group Sort Expert*

Chapter 4 – GROUPING, SUMMARY AND RUNNING TOTAL

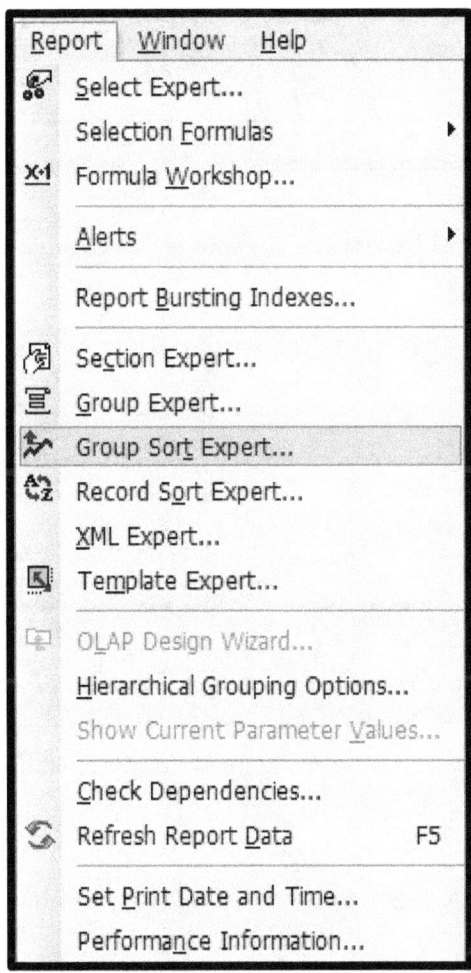

Figure 4.7c – Group Sort Expert.

Chapter 4 – GROUPING, SUMMARY AND RUNNING TOTAL

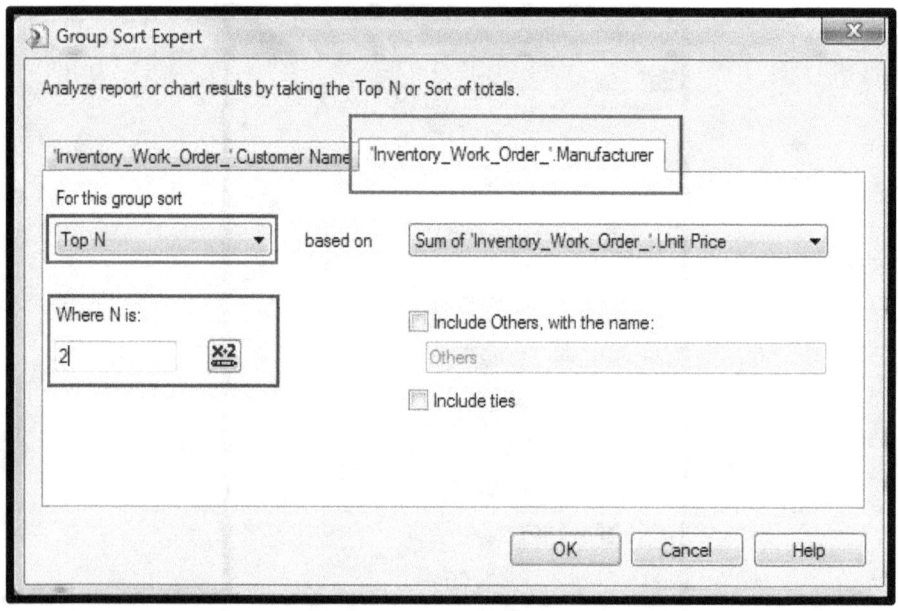

Figure 4.7d – *Select Top N in Group Sort Expert.*

Now, as shown below in figure 4.7e, **Circle Life LLC** has only 2 manufactures listed.

Chapter 4 – GROUPING, SUMMARY AND RUNNING TOTAL

Customer ID	Customer Name	Model	Manufacturer	Serial No#	Unit Price	Invoice Number	Invoice Date
Circle Life LLC							
Alibaba							
224252	Circle Life LLC	NHG335D	Alibaba	AZSF21	$465,487.00	N3564SN	11/30/2012
Jugle boy							
224252	Circle Life LLC	ZV54ZZCV	Jugle boy	SDGSDG21	$46,897.00	N3321574N	03/29/2013

Figure 4.7e – *After sorting to Top 2, the Circle Life LLC report shows only two manufacturers.*

Understanding of Summary

What is Summary? Summary means a shorter version of the original. Summary in Crystal Reports means to add up all the information or data in a group section(s). For example, a summary on a report may display the total of all unit prices in a list, but does not have the unit price for each listed item.

To Insert a **Summary**, you either can select **Insert** from the menu bar, or right click on the selected field and choose **Insert – Summary**. (Make sure you select the field in the **Details** section that you want to summarize), as shown below in figure 4.8a and 4.8b

Chapter 4 – GROUPING, SUMMARY AND RUNNING TOTAL

Figure 4.8a – *Insert a report Summary through the menu bar.*

Chapter 4 – GROUPING, SUMMARY AND RUNNING TOTAL

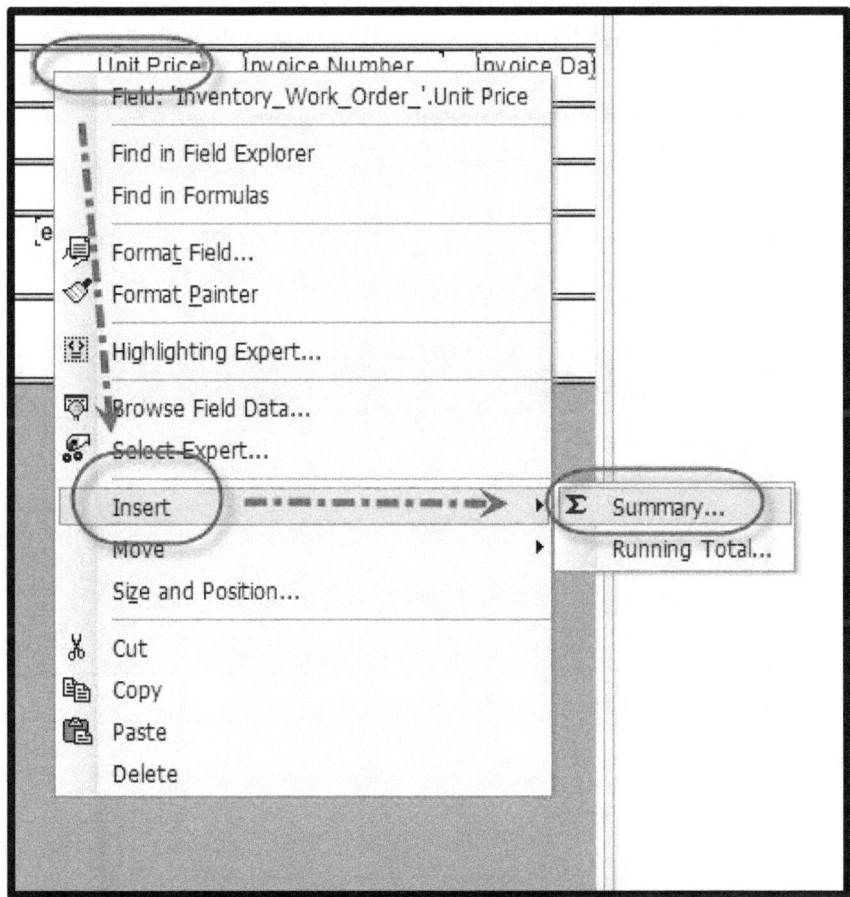

Figure 4.8b *– Right click on the selected field in the Details section, then select "Insert" and "Summary".*

Chapter 4 – GROUPING, SUMMARY AND RUNNING TOTAL

The **Summary function** has options to **Sum, Average, Count,** and manipulate data in many other ways, as shown below in figure 4.9.

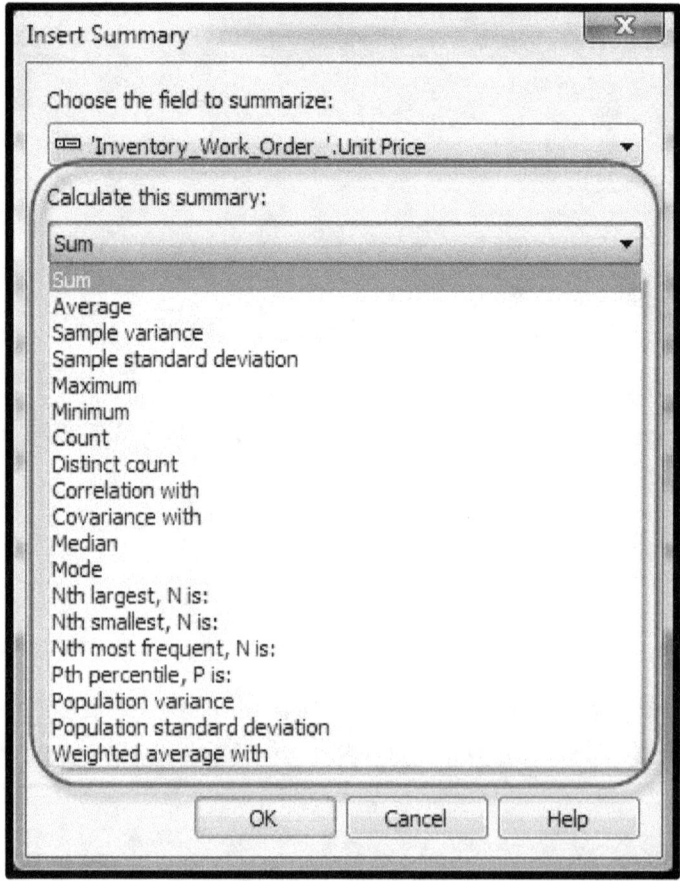

Figure 4.9 – *With Insert Summary, you can do Sum, Average, Maximum, Minimum, Count, and many other useful calculations.*

Chapter 4 – GROUPING, SUMMARY AND RUNNING TOTAL

Summary Example

The **Inventory Work Order** report has been grouped by **Customer Name** and **Manufacturer**. Now, to make the report really useful, let's sum up the **tot**al of all **unit prices** using the **Insert Summary** dialog box.

In **Design** mode, select the **Unit Price** field in the **Details** section. Go to the menu bar and select **Insert** and **Summary**, as shown below in figure 4.10a and 4.10b.

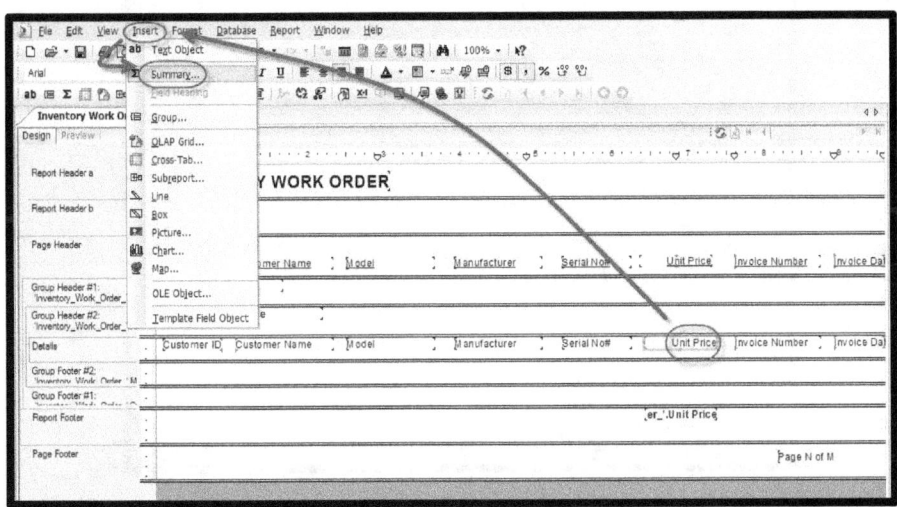

Figure 4.10a – Select the Unit Price field in Details, click Insert on the menu bar, and choose Summary.

Chapter 4 – GROUPING, SUMMARY AND RUNNING TOTAL

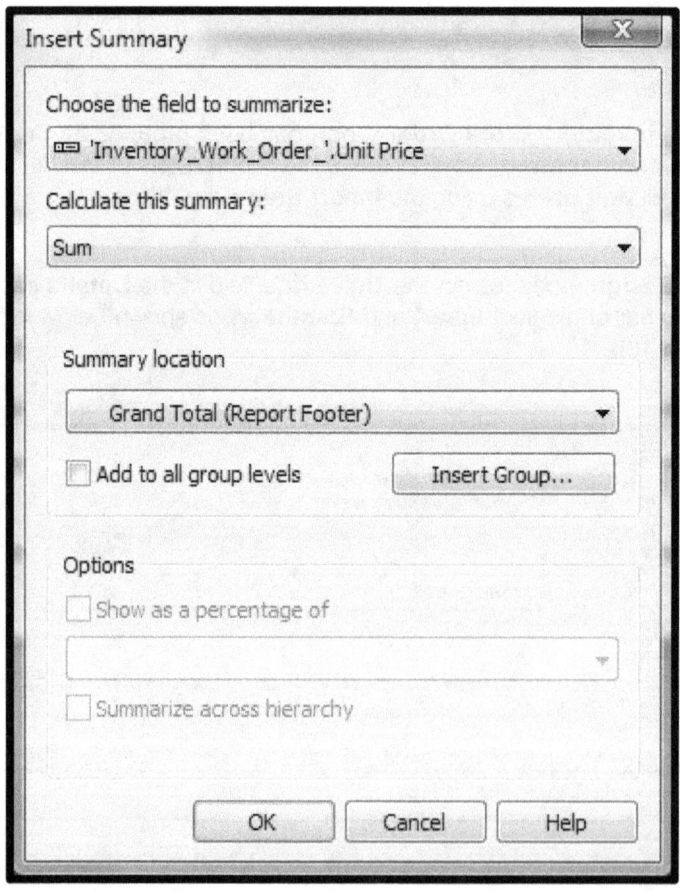

Figure 4.10b – Insert Summary field(s) on the Unit Price.

Chapter 4 – GROUPING, SUMMARY AND RUNNING TOTAL

In the **Insert Summary** window, "**Unit Price**" is the field to be summarized. From the "**Calculate this Summary**" pulldown menu, choose **Sum**. In the **Summary Location** pulldown, select "**Group #2: 'Inventory_Work_Order_'.Manufacturer**" as the summary location, and then click **OK**, as shown below in figure 4.11.

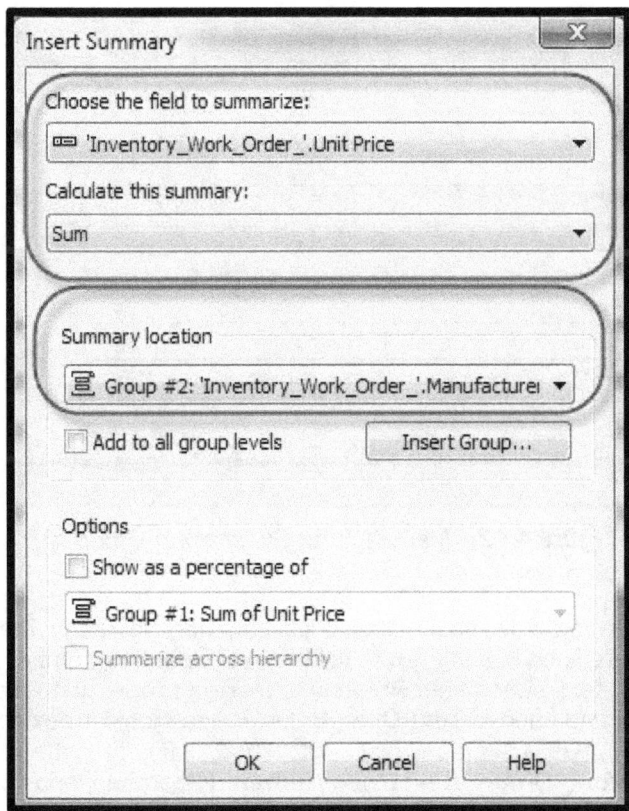

Figure 4.11 – Unit Price is the field to be summarized. Calculate this summary as Sum. Group 2 is the location of the Summary.

Chapter 4 – GROUPING, SUMMARY AND RUNNING TOTAL

Now, each **Group Header #2 (GH2)** has a summary on **Group Footer #2 (GF2)**, as shown below in figure 4.12.

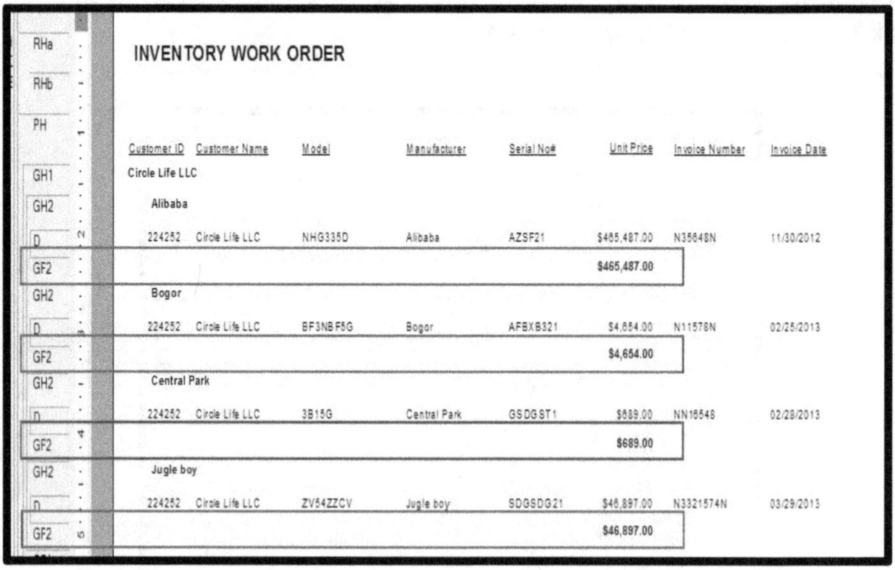

Figure 4.12 – Manufacturer Summary in Group # 2.

The report now has a unit price summary for each manufacturing group, but there is no leading text to tell the user what that number means. To create leading text, switch from **Preview** to **Design mode**, go to the Menu bar, select **Insert,** and choose **Text Object**. Draw a text object box in the **Group Footer #2 (GF2)** area just to the left of the "*Sum of 'Inventory_Work_Order_'.Unit Price (Currency)*" formula, and type **Total by Manufacturer**, as shown below in figure 4.13a, 4.13b and 4.13c.

Chapter 4 – GROUPING, SUMMARY AND RUNNING TOTAL

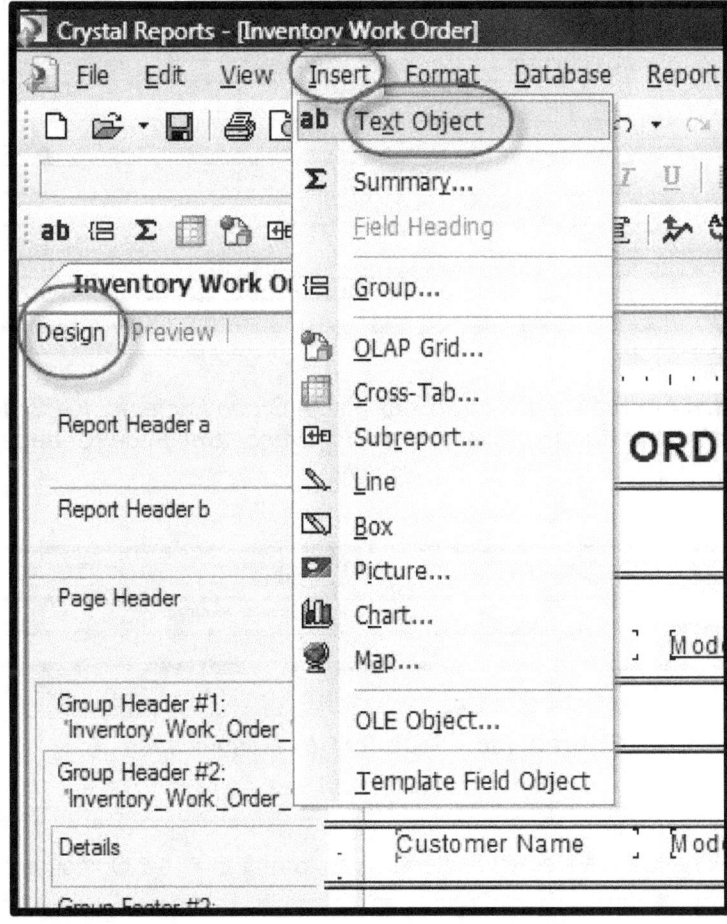

Figure 4.13a – Select Design tab, go to the menu bar, choose Insert, and select Text Object to insert a new Text Object to the report field.

Chapter 4 – GROUPING, SUMMARY AND RUNNING TOTAL

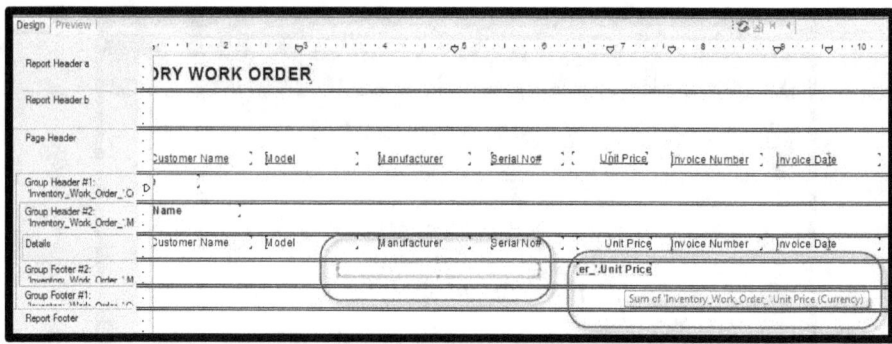

Figure 4.13b – Draw a text object box on the Group Footer #2 (GF2) area to the left of the "Sum of 'Inventory_Work_Order_'.Unit Price (Currency)" formula.

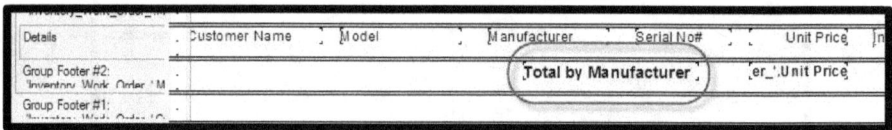

Figure 4.13c – Type Total by Manufacturer.

Note: See Chapter 4 instructions on how to format the Text Object size and position.

To view your work, switch from **Design** tab to **Preview** tab. Group #2 summaries have been added to the report as "**Total by Manufacturer**", as shown below in figure 4.14.

Chapter 4 – GROUPING, SUMMARY AND RUNNING TOTAL

INVENTORY WORK ORDER

Customer ID	Customer Name	Model	Manufacturer	Serial No#	Unit Price	Invoice Number	Invoice Date
Circle Life LLC							
Alibaba							
224252	Circle Life LLC	NHG335D	Alibaba	AZSF21	$465,487.00	N35648N	11/30/2012
			Total by Manufacturer		$465,487.00		
Bogor							
224252	Circle Life LLC	BF3NBF5G	Bogor	AFBXB321	$4,654.00	N11578N	02/25/2013
			Total by Manufacturer		$4,654.00		
Central Park							
224252	Circle Life LLC	3B15G	Central Park	GSDGST1	$689.00	NN16548	02/28/2013
			Total by Manufacturer		$689.00		
Jugle boy							
224252	Circle Life LLC	ZV54ZZCV	Jugle boy	SDGSDG21	$46,897.00	N3321574N	03/29/2013
			Total by Manufacturer		$46,897.00		
Five Suns							
Alibaba							
225422	Five Suns	VB21FG	Alibaba	DSDGG121	$898.00	N33558	02/25/2013
			Total by Manufacturer		$898.00		
Bogor							
225422	Five Suns	XBDFSB13F	Bogor	BFDH1233	$65,498.00	N3235487N	03/06/2013
			Total by Manufacturer		$65,498.00		

Page 1 of 9

Figure 4.14 *– Group #2 summaries have been added to the Inventory Work Order report as "Total by Manufacturer".*

Our report has totals for each manufacturing group within a Customer Name group, but we also need a total of all manufacturing activity by each customer. We can add that now. Go back to **Design** tab, click the Details **Unit Price,** click **Insert,** and select **Summary**, as shown below in figure 4.15.

Chapter 4 – GROUPING, SUMMARY AND RUNNING TOTAL

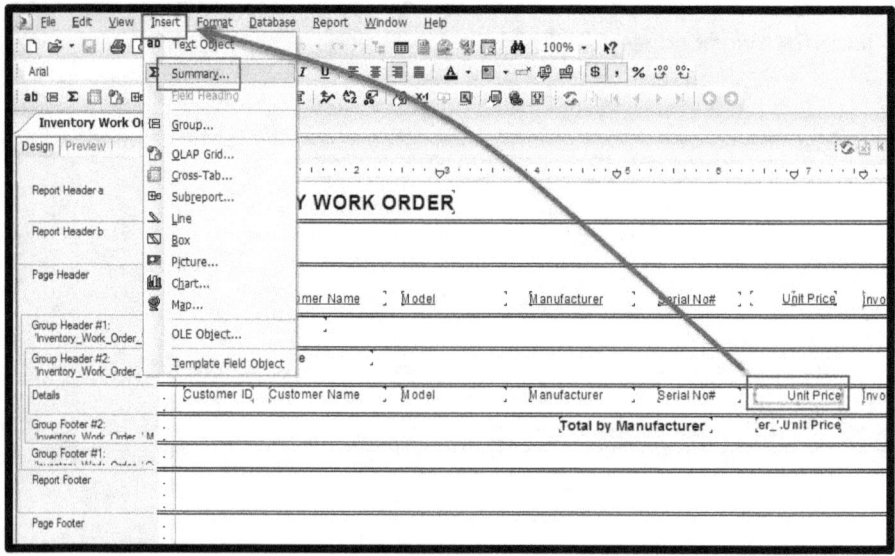

Figure 4.15 – *Select Unit Price in the Details section, click Insert, then Summary.*

Make sure the summarized field is **Unit Price**, the calculate option is **Sum**, and the Summary location is in "**Group #1: 'Inventory_Work_Order_'.Customer Name**", as shown below in figure 4.16. Click **OK**.

Chapter 4 – GROUPING, SUMMARY AND RUNNING TOTAL

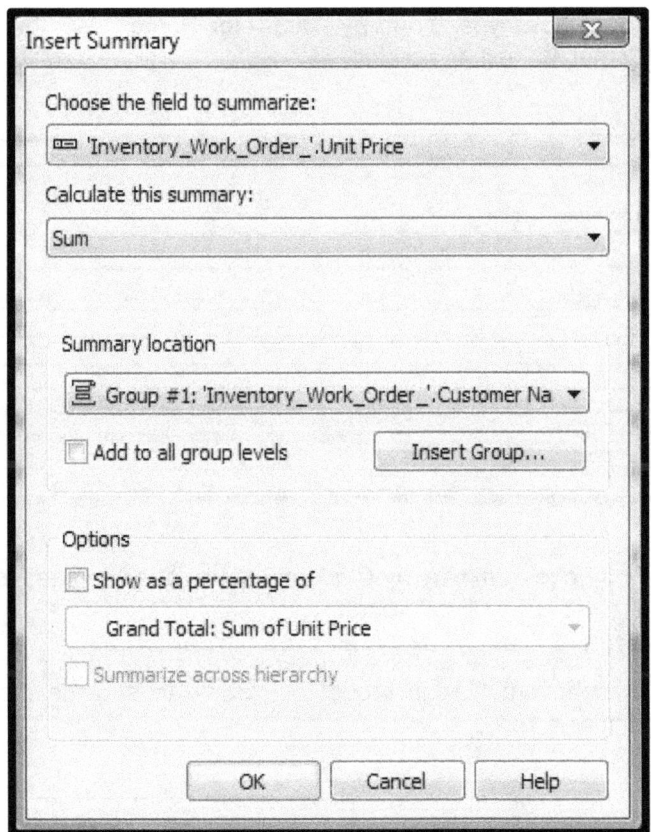

Figure 4.16 – *Inserting Summary of "Group #1 'Inventory_Work_Order_'.Customer Name".*

Repeat the same process for creating leading text as described above in Figures 4.13a, 4.13b and 4.13c. Go to the Menu bar and select **Insert,** then **Text Object**. Draw a new Text Object to the left of our new Unit Price

Chapter 4 – GROUPING, SUMMARY AND RUNNING TOTAL

Summary just added, and type "**Total by Customer Name**", as shown below in figure 4.17. Format the text as needed.

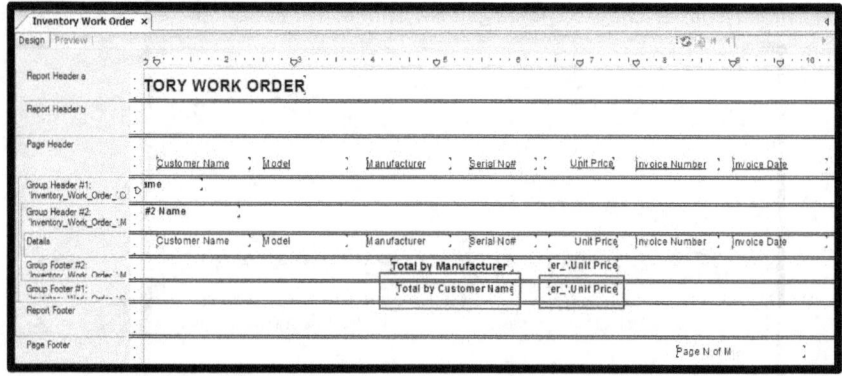

Figure 4.17 – *Unit Price Summary by Customer Name has been added to the report.*

Again, switch from Design mode to Preview to see the report, as shown below in figure 4.18.

Note: The Total by Customer Name is the total of all Unit Prices by Manufacturers.

Chapter 4 – GROUPING, SUMMARY AND RUNNING TOTAL

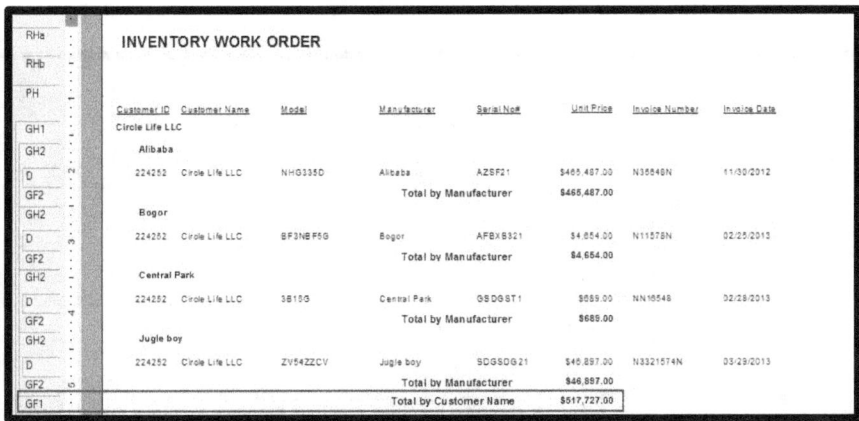

Figure 4.18 – *A Unit Price Summary by Customer Name has been added to the report.*

Running Total

Running Total is just like Summary but you have more options to do field calculations with formulas using the **X-2** button [![X-2]]. In Running Total you can summarize in different ways, as shown below in figure 4.19a and 4.19b.

Chapter 4 – GROUPING, SUMMARY AND RUNNING TOTAL

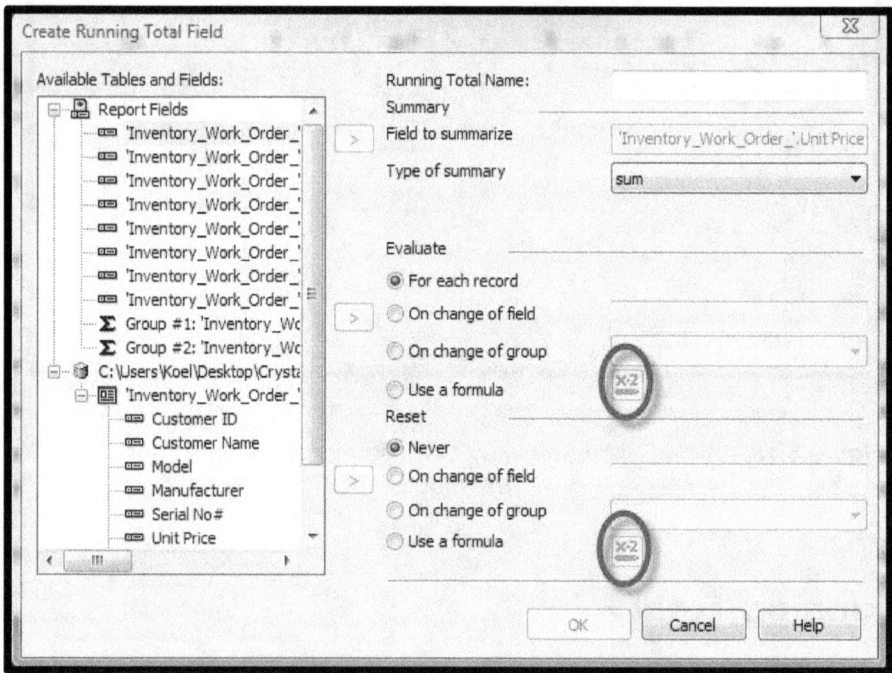

Figure 4.19a – Running Total dialog box.

Chapter 4 – GROUPING, SUMMARY AND RUNNING TOTAL

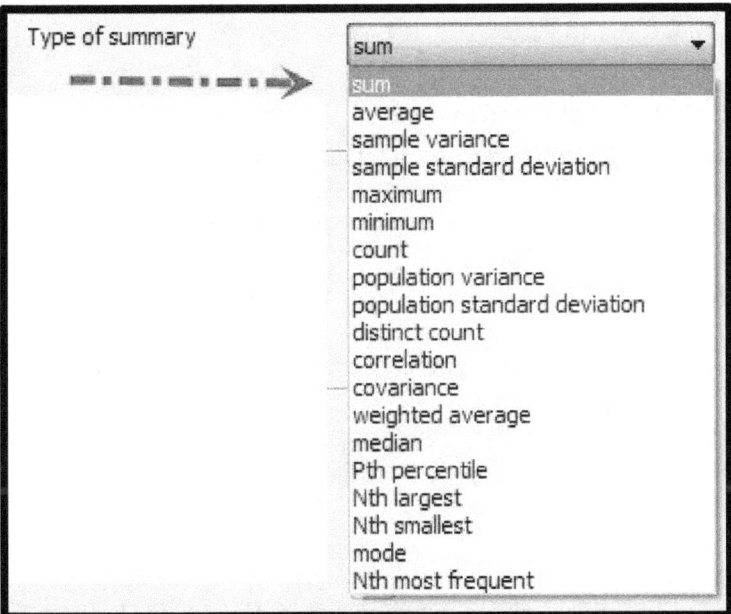

Figure 4.19b – *In Running Total you have many formulas to choose from.*

Before we start using Running Total in the Inventory Work Order report, let's examine the **Create Running Total Field** dialog box:

- **Running Total Name** – This is the field for Running Total name(s) on the report.

Summary

- **Field to summarize** – This option lets you choose the field to be summarized.

- **Type of summary** – Use the pulldown menu to choose a formula type.

Chapter 4 – GROUPING, SUMMARY AND RUNNING TOTAL

Evaluate

Choose your evaluation method:
- **For each record** – Generate a total from all records in the field.

- **On change of field** – Generate a total each time the field changes.

- **On change of Group** – Generate a total each time the group changes.
- **Use a formula** – Apply a formula to the summary value with the X-2 button [$\boxed{x\text{-}2}$]

Reset

- **Never** – Do not reset the summary value. Maintain a Running Total of all records in the field.

- **On change of field** – This option will reset the summary value when the selected field changes.

- **On change of group** – This option will reset the summary value when the selected group changes.
- **Use a formula** – Apply a formula to the reset value with the X-2 button [$\boxed{x\text{-}2}$].

Let's try inserting a **Running Total** in our worksheet. Go to Design tab, right click on the Details **Unit Price**, select **Insert**, and choose **Running Total**, as shown below in figure 4.20.

Chapter 4 – GROUPING, SUMMARY AND RUNNING TOTAL

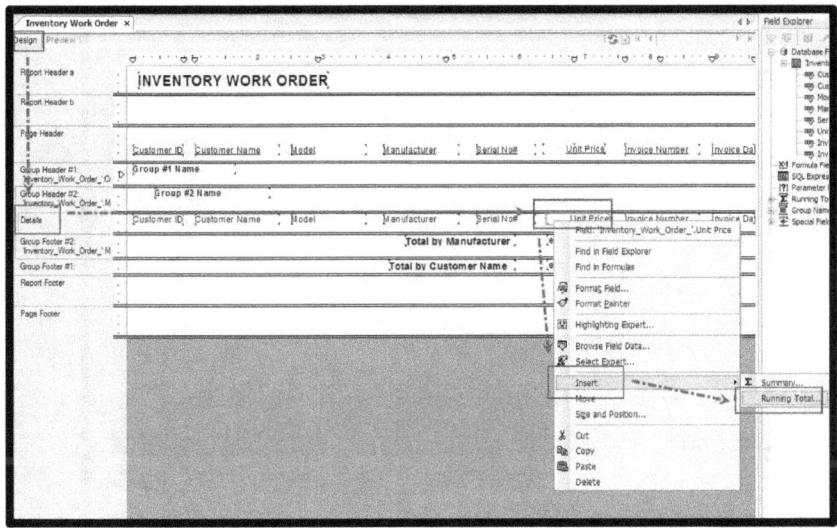

Figure 4.20 – *Insert Running Total from a selected field.*

Type "**Total Unit Price**" in the **Running Total Name** box, keep the "**For each record**" on Evaluate section and "**Never**" on Reset section as the default then click **OK**, as shown below in figure 4.21.

Chapter 4 – GROUPING, SUMMARY AND RUNNING TOTAL

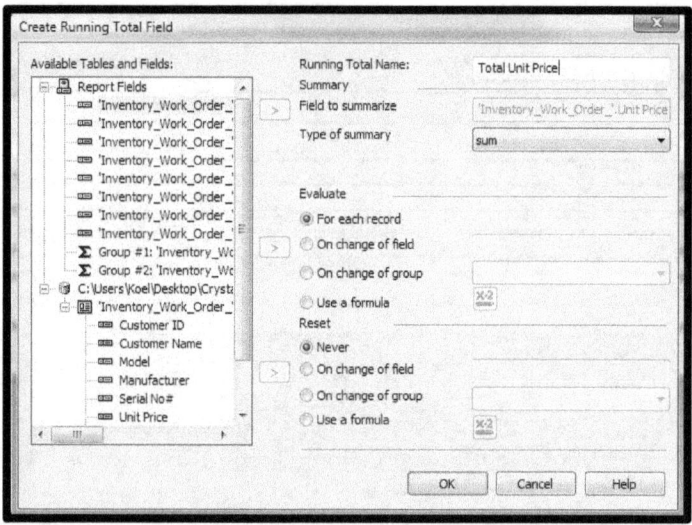

Figure 4.21 – *Total Unit Price.*

Crystal Reports will display the Total Unit Price details and Total Unit Price Header. Since we do not need the Total Unit Price's Header, delete it (select the header, then press delete). Put the **Total Unit Price** details in the Report Footer section and format it to bold.

Insert a Text Object, name it as "**Total Unit Price**" and place it to the left of the new summary value in the Report Footer section.

Now go to the Preview tab to view the last page of the report, as shown below in figure 4.22a, 4.22b and 4.22c.

Chapter 4 – GROUPING, SUMMARY AND RUNNING TOTAL

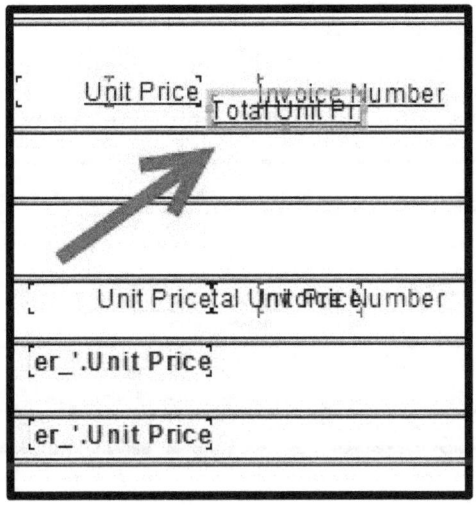

Figure 4.22a – *Select and delete the Total Unit Price header.*

Chapter 4 – GROUPING, SUMMARY AND RUNNING TOTAL

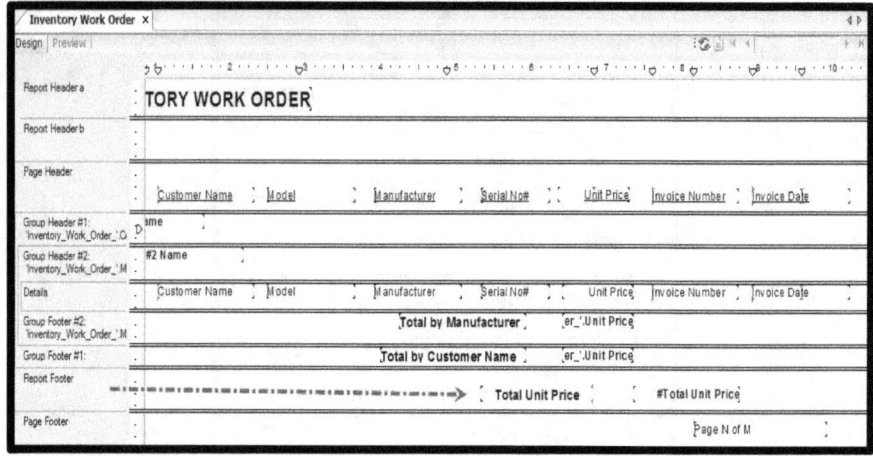

Figure 4.22a – *Place the Total Unit Price in the Report Footer.*

Chapter 4 – GROUPING, SUMMARY AND RUNNING TOTAL

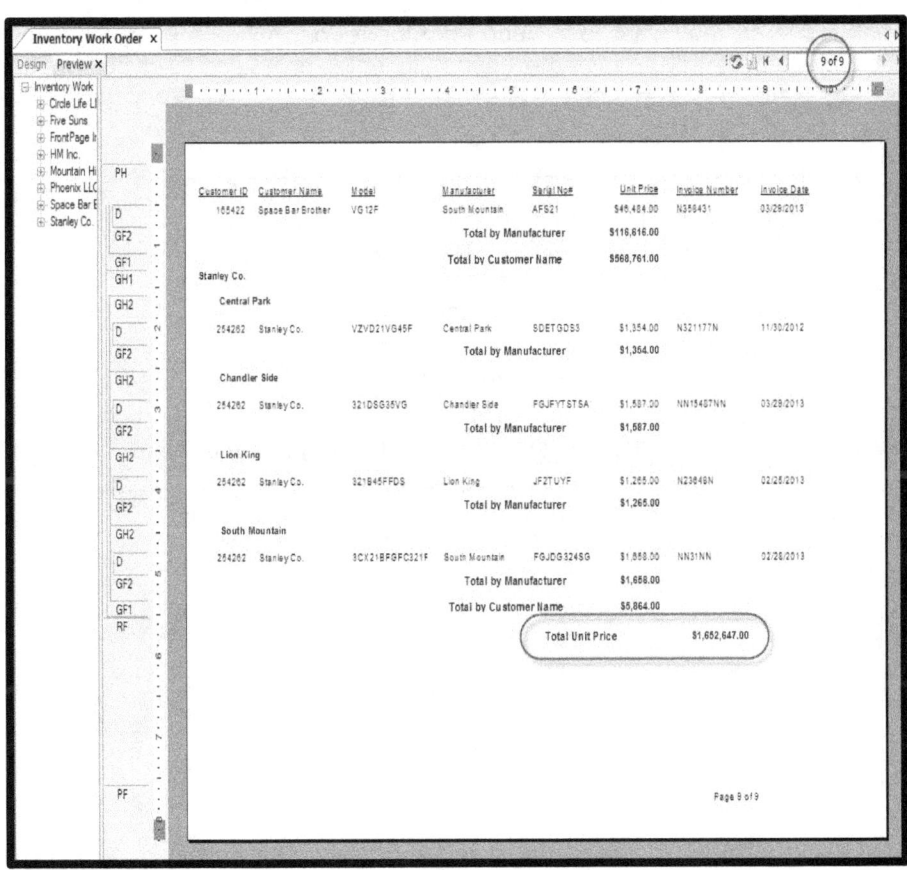

Figure 4.22a – Preview the last page of the report to see the Total Unit Price.

Chapter 5 – PARAMETER

In Crystal Reports, Parameter is a value that controls the report's output data flow, or limits the data to be displayed. In other words, instead of showing everything in the database, the users can specify what data they want to see, or they want to exclude from the report. Once a Parameter has been created, it will prompt the user(s) to enter or select valid criteria for filtering. Here are seven different *Parameter* types.

- **Boolean**: Requires a yes and no or true and false answer
- **Currency**: Requires a dollar amount
- **Date**: Requires an answer in a date format
- **DateTime**: Requires both date and time
- **Number**: Requires a numeric value
- **String**: Requires a text answer
- **Time**: Requires an answer using a time format

In the example below, the user wishes to display only the data for manufacturer "**Bogor**". By establishing "**Manufacturer**" as a Parameter and selecting "**Bogor**" as the criteria, the report will filter out the other manufacturers, and display only the data for "**Bogor**", as shown below in figure 5.1.

Chapter 5 – PARAMETER

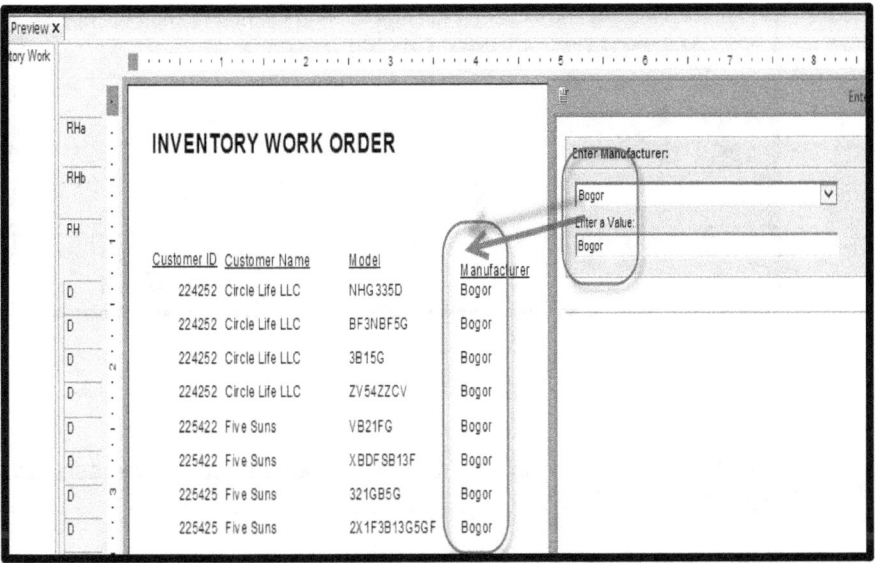

Figure 5.1 – *Displaying the Manufacturer in Bogor Inventory Work Order's only.*

Creating a Parameter Field

To create a *Parameter* field, follow the steps below. Let's do a simple *Parameter* for Customer ID from our Inventory Work Order report.

1. Make sure your report is on **Design** Tab, as shown below in figure 5.2a.

Chapter 5 – PARAMETER

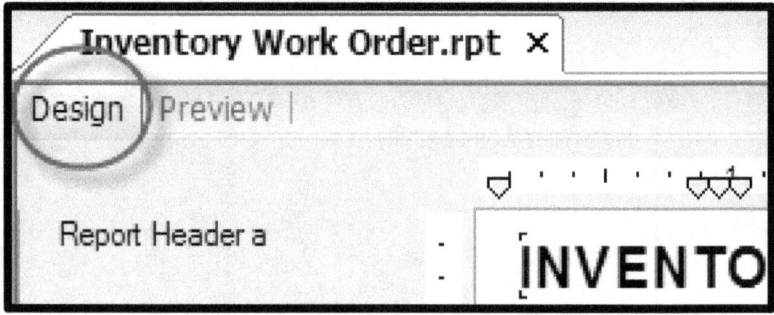

Figure 5.2a – Design Tab

2. Go to **Field Explorer** and right click on **Parameter Fields**, as shown below in figure 5.2b.

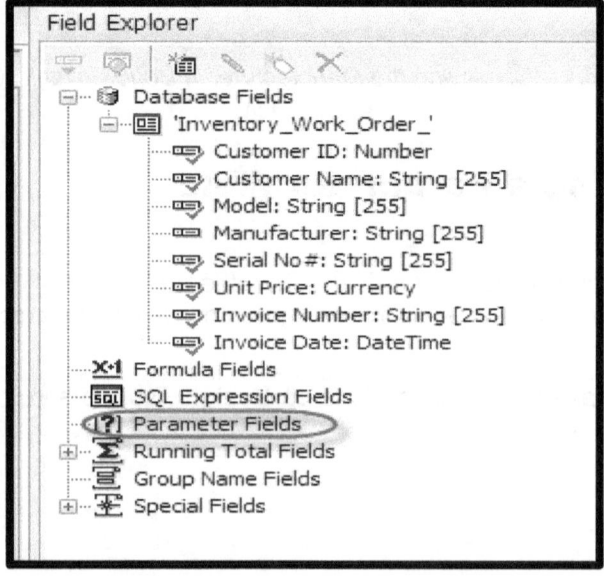

Figure 5.2b – Parameter Fields

Chapter 5 – PARAMETER

3. Select **New** to create a new *Parameter*.

4. In the "**Create New Parameter**" window, Type "**Manufacturer**" into the Name field, as shown below in figure 5.2c.

5. Since the manufacturer names are composed of text characters, choose **String** as the *Parameter* **Type**, as shown below in figure 5.2c.

6. Click the drop down arrow on **Value Field** and select **Manufacturer** from the list, as shown below in figure 5.2c.

7. Click the drop down arrow on **Description Field** and select **Manufacturer** from the list, as shown below in figure 5.2c

8. Click the drop down arrow on **Actions** and select "**Append all database values**" to display all the Customer ID data as Parameter values, as shown below in figure 5.2c.

> **Note:**
>
> In the **Actions**, you use "**Import"** to import a text file when you need to use different value outside from the report database and "**Export**" used to convert all the parameter values to a text file.

9. Set "**Prompt Text**" to "**Enter Manufacturer**:" and set "**Prompt with Description Only**" to "**True**". (*This is optional. You can ignore this value if you don't want the "Description Only" prompt*)

10. Set "**Allow multiple values**" to "**True**". This option will give end users the flexibility to choose more than one value, as shown below in figure 5.2c.

Chapter 5 – PARAMETER

11. Click **OK** and you are done. You can now filter your report by manufacturer name, using the Customer ID **Parameter**, as shown below in figure 5.2c.

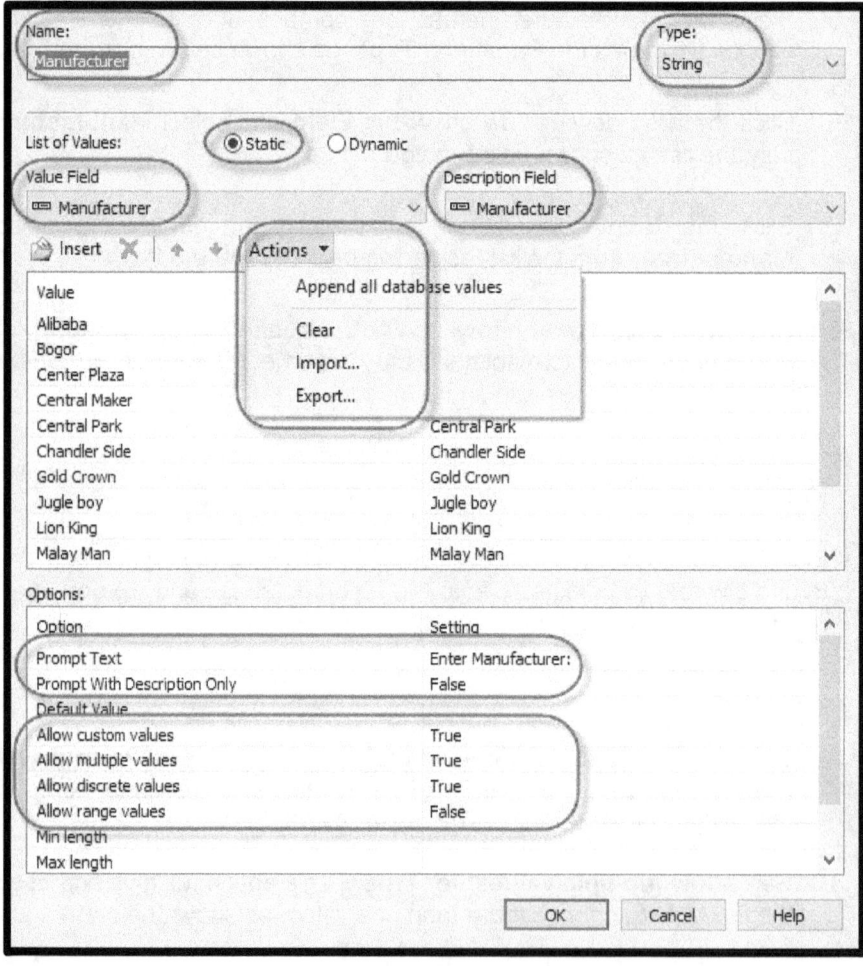

Figure 5.2c – Create New Parameter's window

Chapter 5 – PARAMETER

Notice that there are two different types of Parameters; **Static,** and **Dynamic**.

A **STATIC** Parameter is one that does not take effect immediately and is not directly linked to a database (*the values get updated only when the system is rebooted*).

A **DYNAMIC** Parameter is directly linked to a database, and takes effect immediately in run time.

Activate Parameter

You have just created a new **Manufacturer** Parameter, but it has not been activated and assigned. Active parameter(s) always have a green check mark showing on the left side. Figure 5.3, "**Manufacturer**" does not have the "**green**" color check mark, which means that this Parameter has not yet been placed in the report, or is inactive. The report will not filter correctly until the Parameter has been activated and assigned.

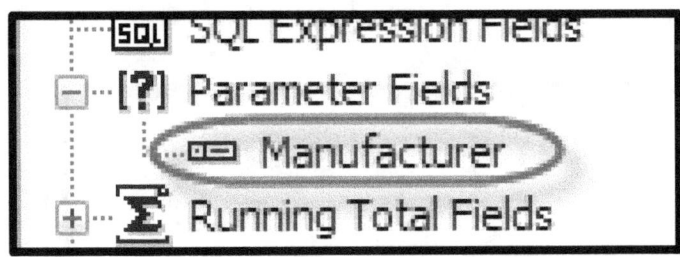

Figure 5.3 – *Manufacturer Parameter has not yet been activated.*

To activate this Parameter, click the word "**Manufacturer**" (which located below "**Parameter's Fields**" in the "**Field Explorer**" dialog box), and drag it to the report area. In this example I placed the Manufacturer's parameter on the page header, as shown below in figure 5.4a.

Chapter 5 – PARAMETER

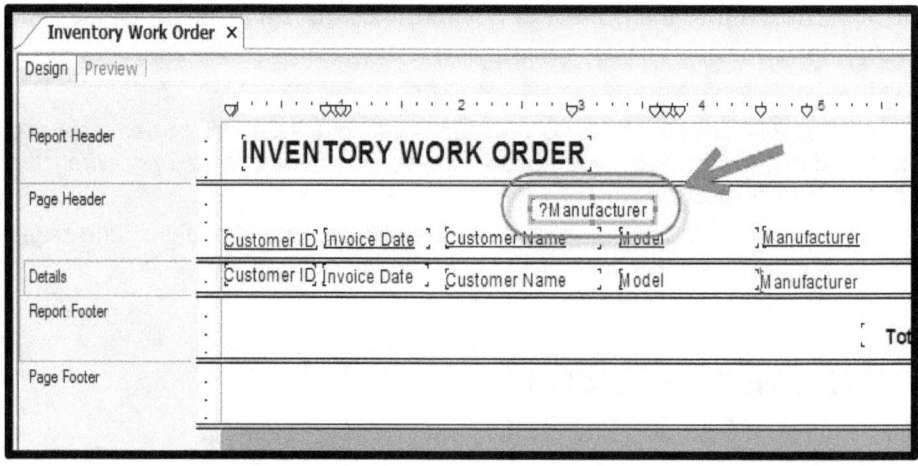

Figure 5.4a – To activate Parameter fields, I placed the Manufacturer's parameter on the page header

As I mentioned above that an active parameter(s) always have a "**green**" color check mark showing on the left side. So Manufacturer's Parameter is now activated, as shown below in figure 5.4b.

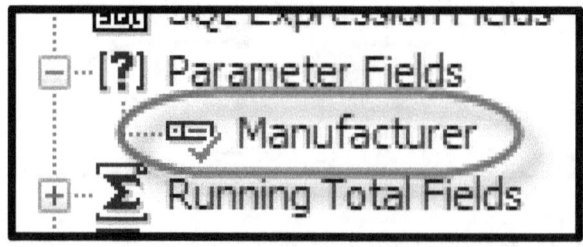

Figure 5.4b – Manufacturer Parameter is showing active

Chapter 5 – PARAMETER

Manufacturer's parameter is now activated but we need to assign this parameter. Remember, parameter is a value that controls the report's output. In order to achieve that, we need to assign this parameter to Manufacturer value from the **Inventory_Work_Order's** database fields.

Assign Parameter

On the top menu bar, simply go to **REPORT** then click **SELECT EXPERT,** choose Manufacturer field then click **OK**, as shown below in figure 5.5a and 5.5b.

Figure 5.5a – *Use **Select Expert** to assign Manufacturer value from the* **Inventory_Work_Order's** *database fields to Manufacturer's parameter*

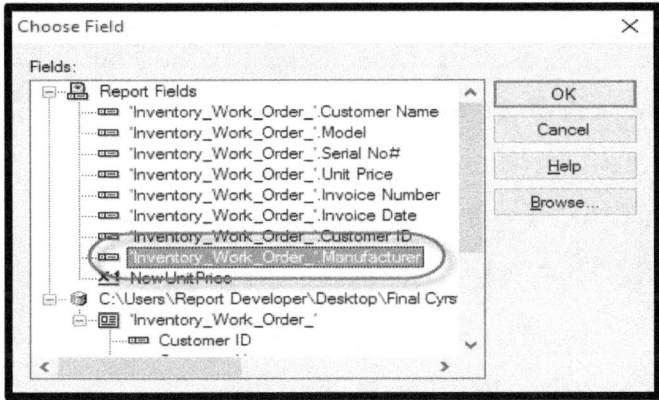

Figure 5.5b – *Select Manufacturer field from Select Expert*

Chapter 5 – PARAMETER

On the **SELECT EXPERT** window of the left drop down box, click and select "**IS EQUAL TO**" then on the right drop down box, click and select **{?Manufacturer}** and click **OK**. You will need to select any manufaturer's values. In this example, I selected "**Bogor**". Click "**Refresh Data**" in order to see the report being updated, as shown below in figure 5.6a, 5.6b and 5.6c.

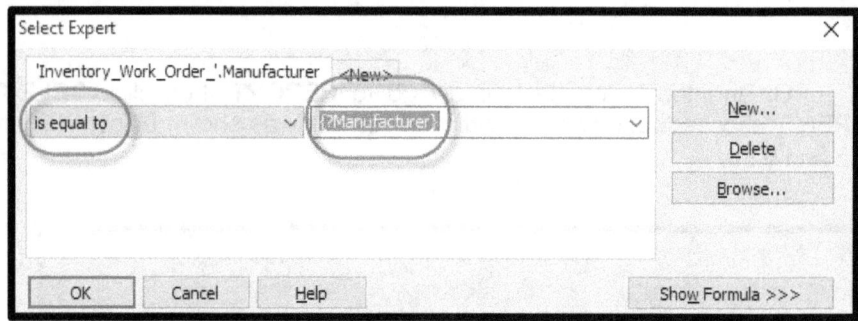

Figure 5.6a – Set Manufacturer field equal to Manufacturer parameter

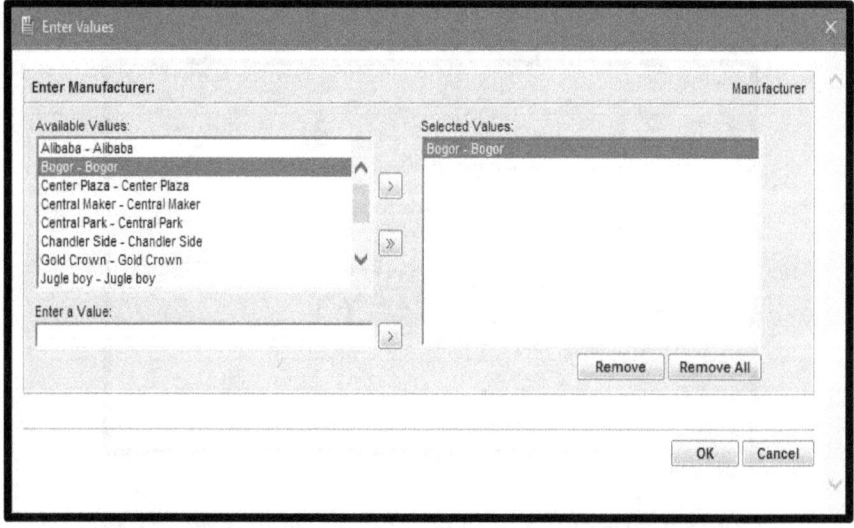

Figure 5.6b – I selected "**Bogor**" as Manufacturer's value

Chapter 5 – PARAMETER

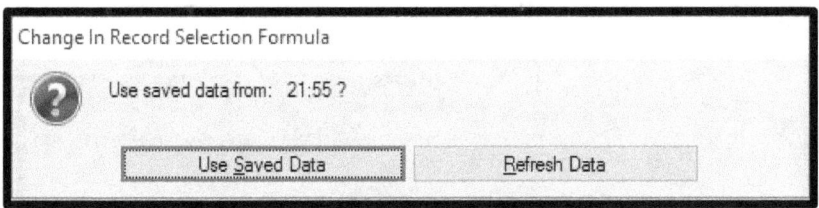

Figure 5.6c – *click "**Refresh Data**" to refresh your data*

As you can see, the Inventory Work Order has filtered out the non-selected manufacturers, and displays only the data for manufacturer "**Bogor**". You can also noticed that the value of Manufacturer parameter of Bogor also printed on top of the report. What you need to do is to supress it, as shown below in figure 5.7a, 5.7b and 5.7c.

INVENTORY WORK ORDER

Bogor

Customer ID	Invoice Date	Customer Name	Model	Manufacturer
116252	11/30/2012	FrontPage Inc.	LLDFE2	Bogor
224252	02/25/2013	Circle Life LLC	BF3NBF5G	Bogor
133154	02/25/2013	Mountain Hill	JJDLK1210M	Bogor
116252	02/25/2013	FrontPage Inc.	JDYDCCX	Bogor
133154	02/26/2013	Mountain Hill	213HDSBFHBZ	Bogor
225422	03/08/2013	Five Suns	XBDFSB13F	Bogor
154542	03/18/2013	Space Bar Brother	JHK1231	Bogor
133154	03/29/2013	Mountain Hill	MNBJH2121	Bogor

Figure 5.7a – *Inventory Work Order report, filtered by Parameter*

Chapter 5 – PARAMETER

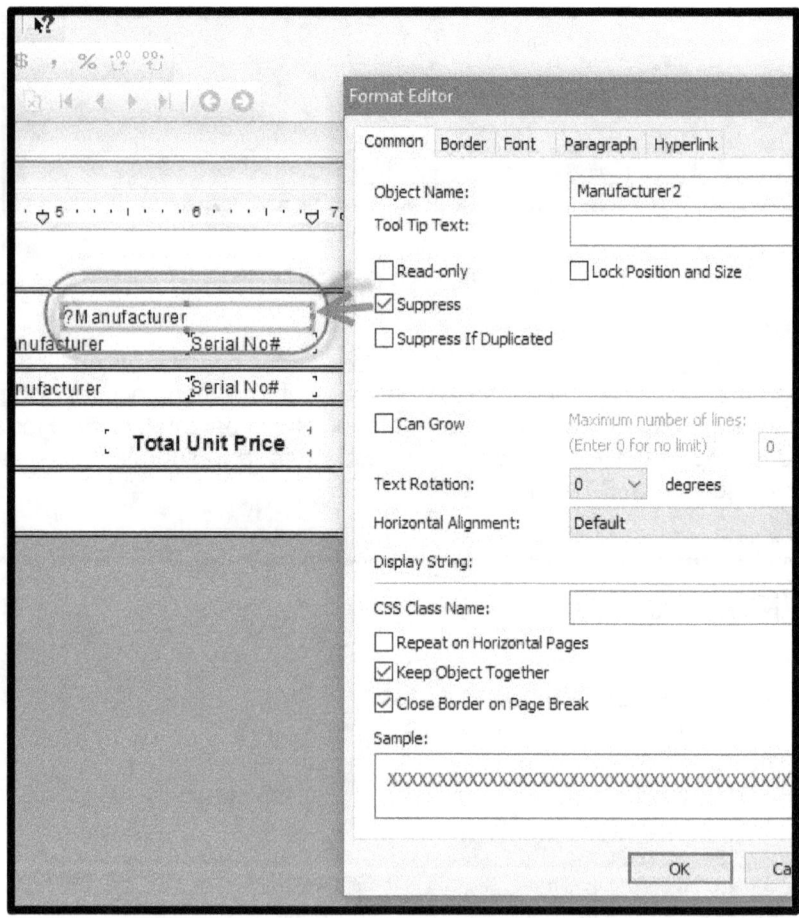

Figure 5.7b – Suppress the manufacturer parameter

Chapter 5 – PARAMETER

INVENTORY WORK ORDER

Customer ID	Invoice Date	Customer Name	Model	Manufacturer
116252	11/30/2012	FrontPage Inc.	LLDFE2	Bogor
224252	02/25/2013	Circle Life LLC	BF3NBF5G	Bogor
133154	02/25/2013	Mountain Hill	JJDLK1210M	Bogor
116252	02/25/2013	FrontPage Inc.	JDYDCCX	Bogor
133154	02/26/2013	Mountain Hill	213HDSBFHBZ	Bogor
225422	03/08/2013	Five Suns	XBDFSB13F	Bogor
154542	03/18/2013	Space Bar Brother	JHK1231	Bogor
133154	03/29/2013	Mountain Hill	MNBJH2121	Bogor

Figure 5.7c – *Inventory Work Order where the manufacturer is equal to Bogor*

Congratulations! You have created a parameter to filter the result set on your report. Manufacturer's parameter is now able to controls the report's output.

Earlier, in chapter 1, I talked about how end users can export from Crystal Reports to different formats, but the most frequently used formats are Adobe.pdf or Microsoft Excel.

Now, let me show you how to use parameters to specify which format type to use when exporting your report. This parameter is useful when you have a fairly complex Crystal Report, and you need to export to both Adobe and Excel.

Are you ready?

Chapter 5 – PARAMETER

P_Excel Parameter

Let's create another new parameter called "**P_Excel**". Enter the value manually as follows:

1. In the "**Create New Parameter**" dialog box, enter **"Pdf format"** as your PDF description.

2. Enter **"Excel Spreadsheet"** as your Excel description.

In the Options section:

1. Set "**Prompt Text**" to "**What report format? (Pdf or Excel)**".

2. Set "**Prompt With Description Only**" to **"True"**.
   (See figure 5.8)

Chapter 5 – PARAMETER

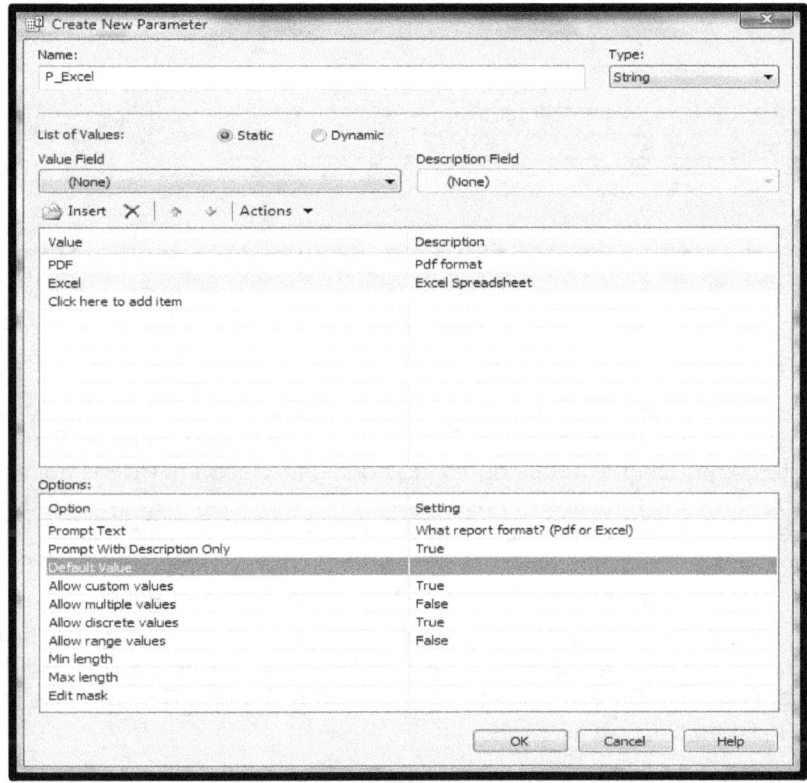

Figure 5.8 – *Creating a new parameter called P_Excel*

In this example, our Inventory Work Order report has two groups in the Sections list. They are group by Customer ID (Group # 1) and Invoice Date (Group # 2). In the Row's section, this report has the Total of the Unit Price as well, as shown below in figure 5.9.

Chapter 5 – PARAMETER

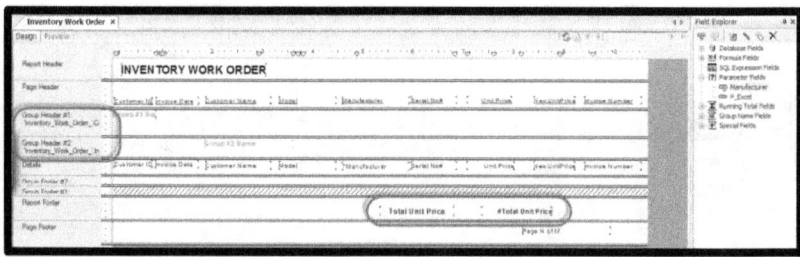

Figure 5.9 – *Inventory Work Order has two groups and Total Unit Price*

The end user needs to run this report in two different formats. As a PDF file, with all the grouping and Total Unit Price counts, and as an Excel file, with no grouping or Total counts. Exporting the report to PDF is not an issue because the output will appear exactly like it does in the *Crystal Report*. If you export this report to Excel, however, your data will contain column headers and group totals that were created within *Crystal Reports,* and do not belong in the Excel version. These will need to be filtered or edited out.

We can fix this problem by creating a new *Crystal Reports* "**Section**" that will export only the data that is needed in the Excel spreadsheet. To do this, right click on "**Detail**", and then select "**Insert Section Below**", as shown below in figure 5.10.

Chapter 5 – PARAMETER

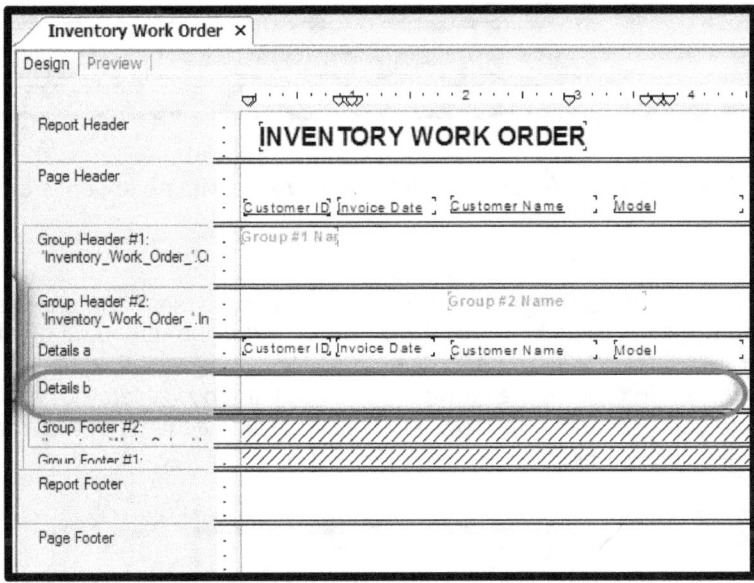

Figure 5.10 – Insert a Detail section

Click and drag all the fields you need to the **"Details b"** section and place each field side by side with no space in between fields (extra spaces between fields will create empty columns in the spreadsheet), as shown below in figure 5.11a and 5.11b.

Figure 5.11a – Click and drag all the fields with no space in between

Chapter 5 – PARAMETER

Figure 5.11b – Place each field side by side with no space in between fields

Now, right click anywhere in the report sections' area and choose **"Section Expert"**. Highlight "**Details b**" in the "**Sections**" menu, and select the "*Suppress (No Drill-Down)*" X-2 button. Next, insert the formula **{?p_Excel} <> 'Excel'** where prompted. This command will force Crystal Reports to suppress the entire row and columns/fields if the output format is not Excel, as shown below in figure 5.12a, 5.12b and 5.12c.

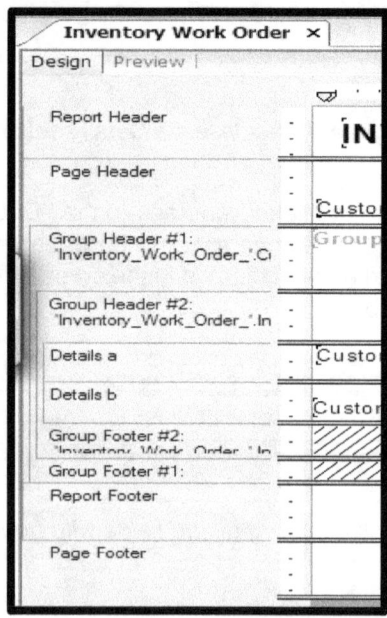

Figure 5.12a – Sections area on the report

Chapter 5 – PARAMETER

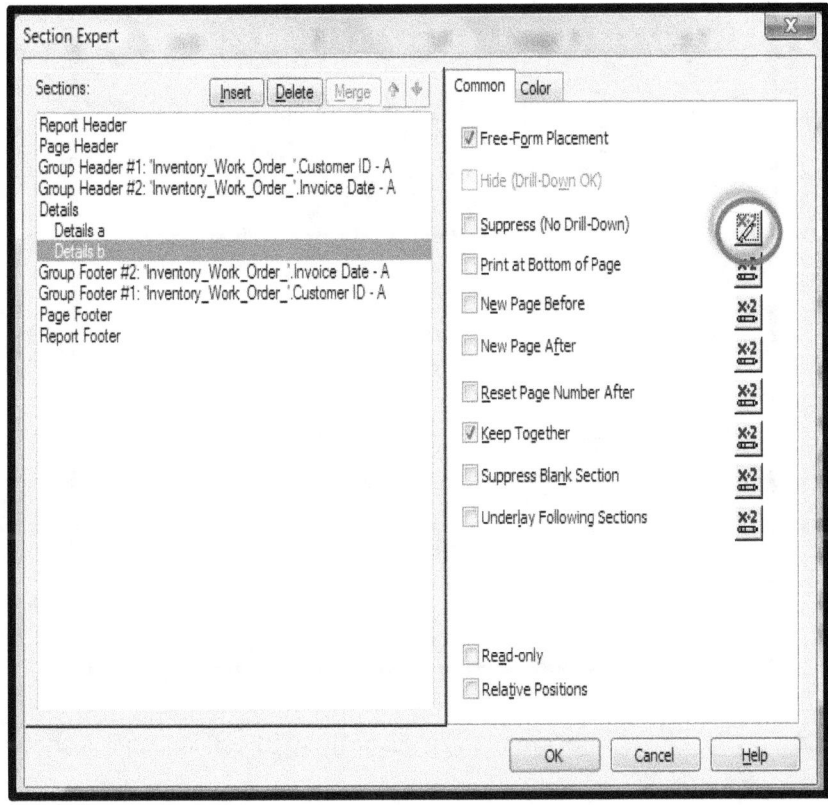

Figure 5.12b – *In Details b - Select the "Suppress (No Drill-Down)" X-2 button*

Chapter 5 – PARAMETER

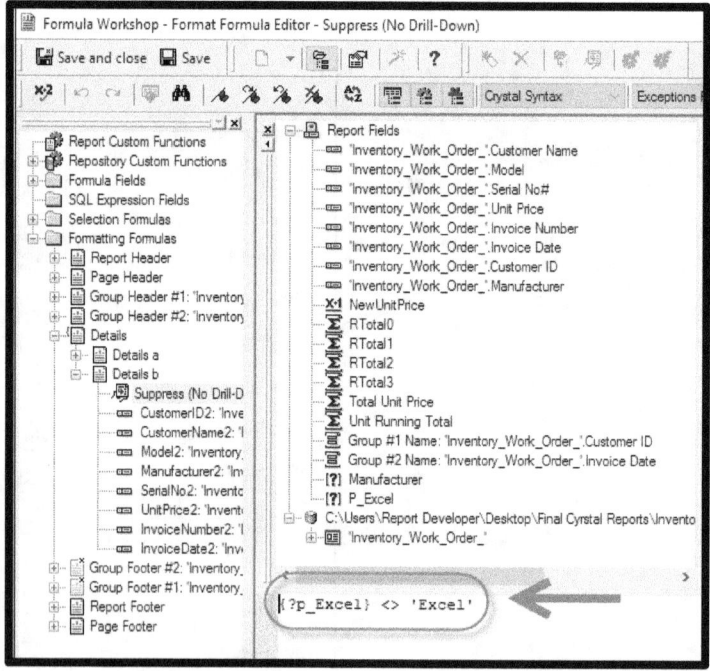

Figure 5.12c – Insert the formula **{?p_Excel} <> 'Excel'** in Detail B section

Do the same thing to all the other sections by adding the formula of **{?p_Excel} = 'Excel'** except to the **Report Header**. This will suppress all other sections, groupings from the output, and send only data to the Excel report (except for the Report Header).

Let's preview the report and select Excel format. Click the "**Refresh**" (**F5**) button to refresh the report, select "**Prompt for new parameter values**", and select **"Excel Spreadsheet"** format, as shown below in figure 5.13a, 5.13b, 5.13c and 5.13d)

Chapter 5 – PARAMETER

Note: The formula of **{?p_Excel} <> 'Excel'** in the "*Suppress (No Drill-Down)*" **X-2** button means to suppress the section when exporting report to other formats except to excel format while the formula of **{?p_Excel} = 'Excel'** in the "*Suppress (No Drill-Down)*" X-2 button means to suppress the section when exporting to excel except other to formats.

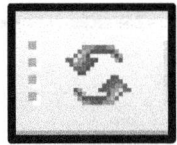

Figure 5.13a – Refresh button to refresh the report

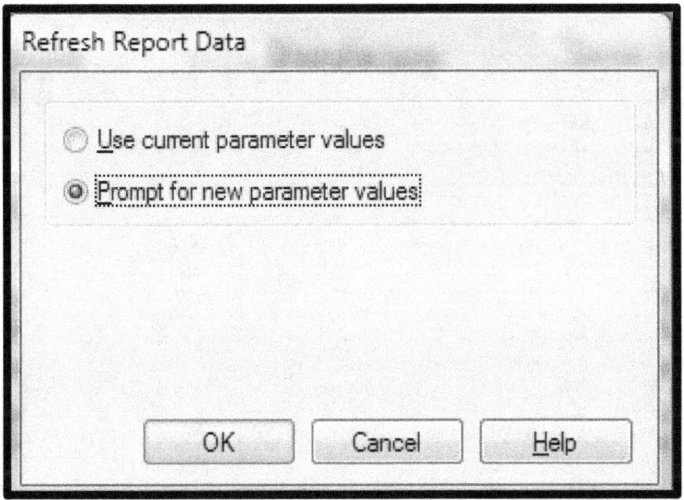

Figure 5.13b – Prompt for new parameter values

Chapter 5 – PARAMETER

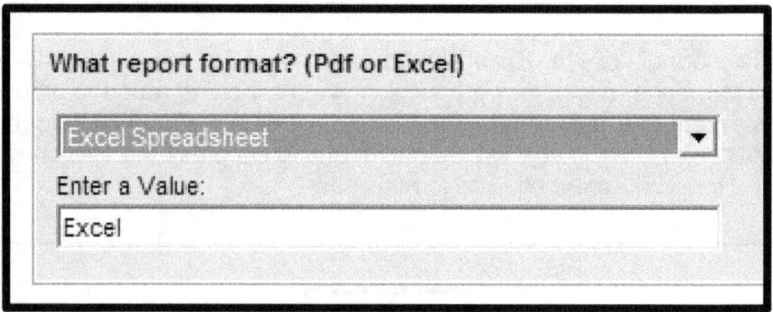

Figure 5.13c – Select viewing format

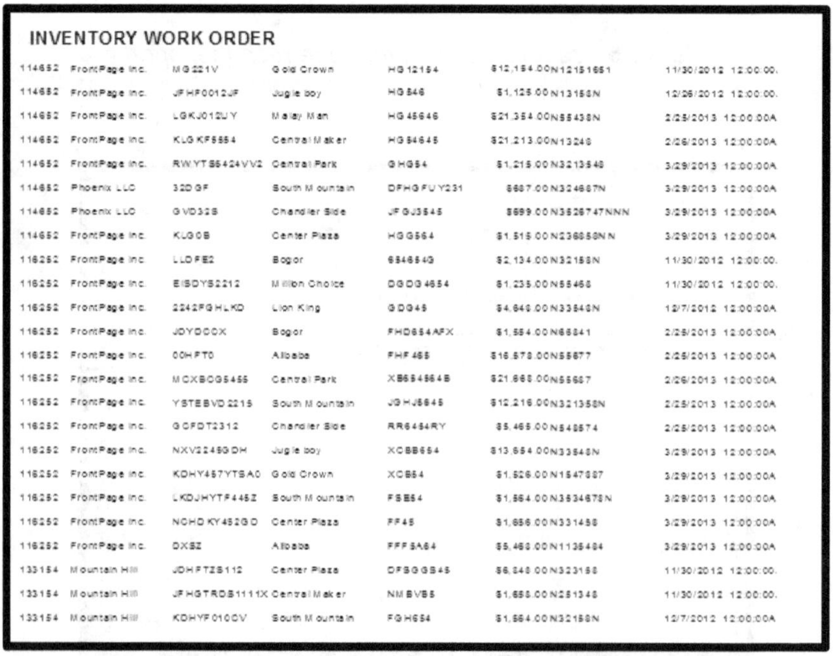

Figure 5.13d – Excel format with no grouping and Total Unit Price options

Chapter 5 – PARAMETER

Select "**Export**", and then "**Microsoft Excel 97-2000 – Data only (XLS)**" and Destination "**Application**" (view only) in the Export box, and click "**OK**". Next, select "**Custom: Data is exported according to selected options**" and click "**OK**", as shown below in figure 5.14a, 5.14b and 5.14c).

Figure 5.14a – Export button

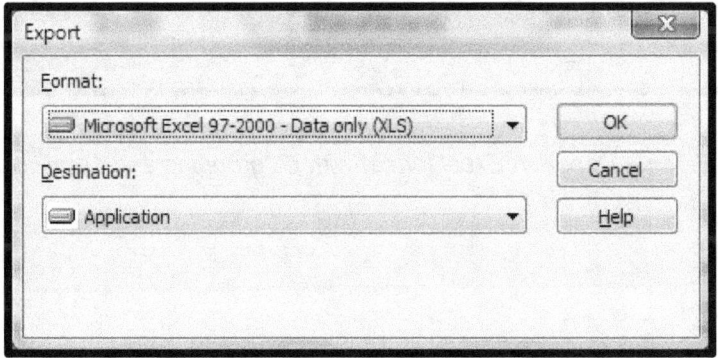

Figure 5.14b – Export box

Chapter 5 – PARAMETER

A	B	C	D	E	F	G	H
INVENTORY WORK ORDER							
114652	FrontPage Inc.	MG221V	Gold Crown	HG12154	$12,154.00	N12151651	11/30/2012 12:00:00 AM
114652	FrontPage Inc.	JFHF0012JF	Jugle boy	HG546	$1,125.00	N13158N	12/26/2012 12:00:00 AM
114652	FrontPage Inc.	LGKJ012UY	Malay Man	HG45646	$21,354.00	N55438N	2/25/2013 12:00:00 AM
114652	FrontPage Inc.	KLGKF5554	Central Maker	HG54645	$21,213.00	N13248	2/26/2013 12:00:00 AM
114652	FrontPage Inc.	RWYTS5424VV2	Central Park	GHG54	$1,215.00	N3213548	3/29/2013 12:00:00 AM
114652	Phoenix LLC	32DGF	South Mountain	DFHGFUY231	$687.00	N324687N	3/29/2013 12:00:00 AM
114652	Phoenix LLC	GVD32S	Chandler Side	JFGJ3545	$699.00	N3526747NNN	3/29/2013 12:00:00 AM
114652	FrontPage Inc.	KLG0B	Center Plaza	HGG564	$1,515.00	N236858NN	3/29/2013 12:00:00 AM
116252	FrontPage Inc.	LLDFE2	Bogor	654654G	$2,134.00	N32158N	11/30/2012 12:00:00 AM
116252	FrontPage Inc.	EISDYS2212	Million Choice	DGDG4654	$1,235.00	N55468	11/30/2012 12:00:00 AM
116252	FrontPage Inc.	2242FGHLKD	Lion King	GDG45	$4,648.00	N33548N	12/7/2012 12:00:00 AM
116252	FrontPage Inc.	JDYDCCX	Bogor	FHD654AFX	$1,554.00	N66841	2/25/2013 12:00:00 AM
116252	FrontPage Inc.	00HFT0	Alibaba	FHF465	$16,578.00	N55677	2/25/2013 12:00:00 AM
116252	FrontPage Inc.	MCXBCG5455	Central Park	XB654564B	$21,668.00	N55687	2/26/2013 12:00:00 AM
116252	FrontPage Inc.	YSTEBVD2215	South Mountain	JGHJ5645	$12,216.00	N321358N	2/25/2013 12:00:00 AM
116252	FrontPage Inc.	GCFDT2312	Chandler Side	RR6454RY	$5,465.00	N548574	2/25/2013 12:00:00 AM
116252	FrontPage Inc.	NXV2245GDH	Jugle boy	XCBB654	$13,654.00	N33548N	3/29/2013 12:00:00 AM
116252	FrontPage Inc.	KDHY457YTSA0	Gold Crown	XCB54	$1,526.00	N15478887	3/29/2013 12:00:00 AM
116252	FrontPage Inc.	LKDJHYTF445Z	South Mountain	FSE54	$1,564.00	N3534678N	3/29/2013 12:00:00 AM

Figure 5.14c – *Report in Excel format with no grouping and Total Unit Price*

Chapter 6 – FORMULAS and FUNCTIONS

Now that you have an extensive understanding on the developmental and formatting process of reports, I'd like to share some pointers about formula and functions. It's important to note that given the expansive and vastly customizable nature of this topic, this chapter will only provide you with a basic foundational knowledge such as how to build formulas within a report. At the end of this chapter, I provided some basic formula samples.

What Is Formula?

Formula(s) is a code written within a report(s) that enables various attributes to be modified, and it gets activated whenever the report(s) refreshed. The function of a formula(s) is to compile the values that are not available in a database to help the user(s) to analyze the data correctly display.

A simple basic report that does just display the data from a database does not need formula but an elaborate report(s) that requires a lot of changes need formulas.

> **Note**: Formula in Crystal Report is not case sensitive.

Create a Simple Formula

Let's do a simple formula for now then I will introduce to you more about the Formulas and Functions in this chapter. In this example, I am going to use the **Unit Price** field to do our first formula example. Let's assume, for each Unit Price, we would like to add 5% on top of the current price.

Chapter 6 – FORMULAS and FUNCTIONS

So follow these steps:
1. Open your *Field Explorer*
2. Right click on "**Formula Fields**"
3. Select "**New**"
4. Type a name for your Formula. In this simple formula, I am going to name the formula as "**NewUnitPrice**"
5. Click "**OK**", as shown below in figure 6.1.

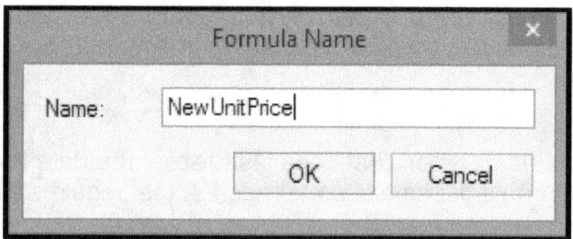

Figure 6.1 – Formula Name

    The Formula Editor appears and ready for us to create our first Crystal Reports' formula. Inside the red rectangle's line (Formula text area) is the area where we write the formula, as shown below in figure 6.2.

Chapter 6 – FORMULAS and FUNCTIONS

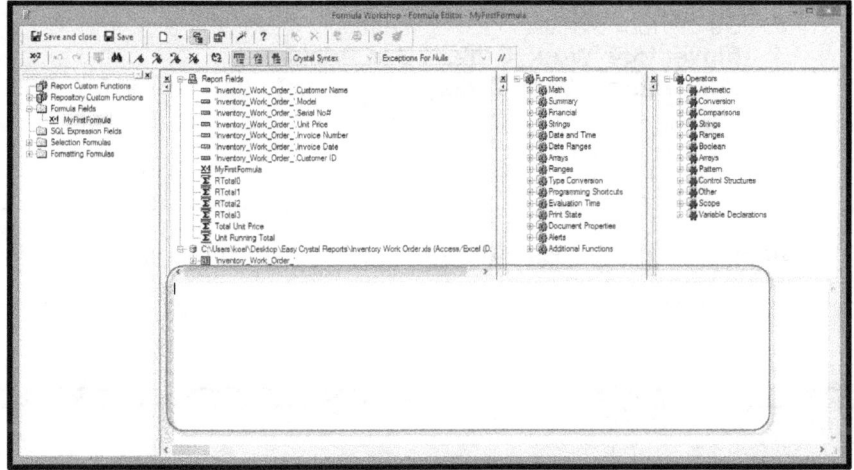

Figure 6.2 – *Formula Editor to create Crystal Reports' formula*

From the Formula Editor's window:

1. Click and drag the ***Inventory_Work_Order.Unit Price*** to the formula field area (*red rectangle area*)
2. Type "**+**" sign (*add*) - or you can use the Arithmetic's operator "**Add**" from Operators' field in the Formula Editor window
3. Type open **Parentheses** "(" sign
4. Click and drag the ***Inventory_Work_Order.Unit Price***
5. Type "*****" sign (*multiply*) - or you can use the Arithmetic's operator "**Multiply**" from Operators' field in the Formula Editor window
6. Type *0.05* (5%)

Chapter 6 – FORMULAS and FUNCTIONS

7. Type close **Parentheses ")"** sign
8. So the formula would looks like this:
   {'Inventory_Work_Order_'.Unit Price} + ({'Inventory_Work_Order_'.Unit Price} * 0.05) – See figure 6.3 below.

> **Note:** All Database fields are surrounded by { } – curly bracket sign

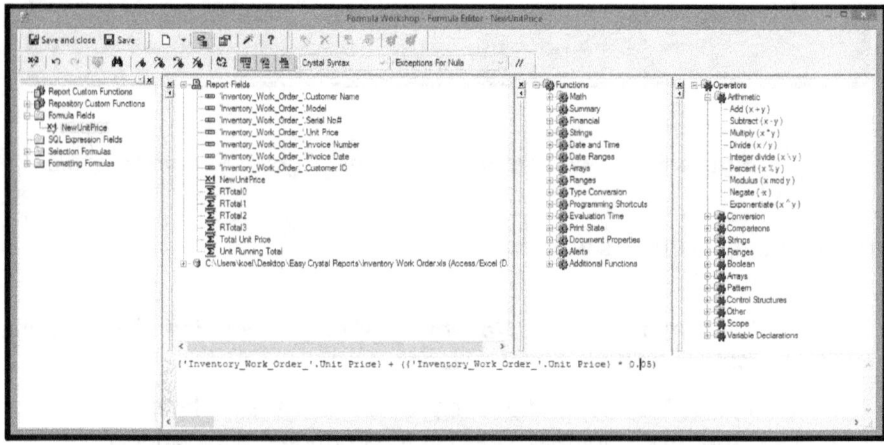

Figure 6.3 *– New Unit Price formula: {'Inventory_Work_Order_'.Unit Price} + ({'Inventory_Work_Order_'.Unit Price} * 0.05)*

Now, let's check our first formula by clicking the "**X+2**". The "**X+2**" will tell us if there are any errors with our formula or not. It is a good practice that we always use the **X+2** (Check's button) to check any formulas that we create to make sure they are correct before we save and close the Formula Editor.

Chapter 6 – FORMULAS and FUNCTIONS

Great news! The **X+2** (check's button) indicated that there is **NO ERROR** with our first formula. Let's click "**Save and Close**" in the Formula Editor. Now you have created the first formula with no error. **Good job!** See below in figure 6.4a and 6.4b.

Figure 6.4a – No errors found on the Formula

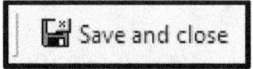

Figure 6.4b – Save and close button on the top left corner of the Formula Editor.

Insert and use your Formulas

As you can see in the Field Explorer, we do now have our first formula called "**NewUnitPrice**." Now from the Inventory Work Order report, click the Design tab to activate the Design mode. Click and drag the "**NewUnitPrice**" to the Details section next to the Unit Price's field, as shown below in figure 6.5a and 6.5b.

Chapter 6 – FORMULAS and FUNCTIONS

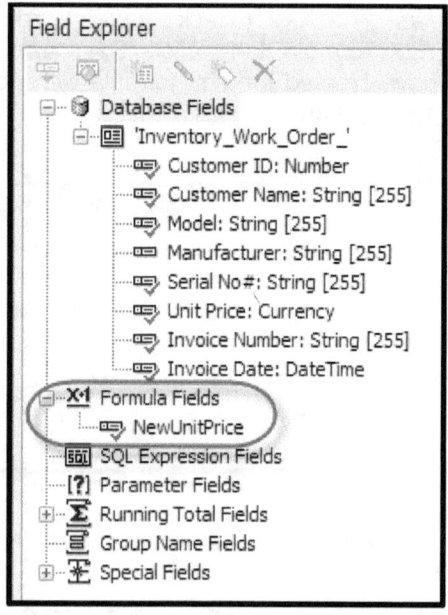

Figure 6.5a – *We have created our new first formula called "NewUnitPrice"*

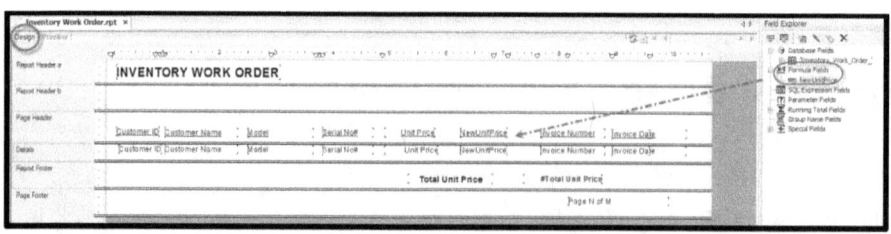

Figure 6.5b – *Activate Design tab, click and drag **NewUnitPrice** to Details section.*

Chapter 6 – FORMULAS and FUNCTIONS

Now, let's preview the Inventory Work Order report and check whether the New Unit Price's amount has correctly increased 5% from the original Unit Price amount or not. Let's pick the first original Unit Price of Customer: **FrontPage Inc.** that has Model: **LLDFE2** and Serial: **654654G** is $2,134.00. Adding 5% to the initial price would make a New Unit Price equal to: ($2,134.00 + ($2,134 * 5%)) = $2,134 + $106.70 = $2,240.70. So this result has concluded that our New Unit Price value is correct, as shown below in figure 6.6.

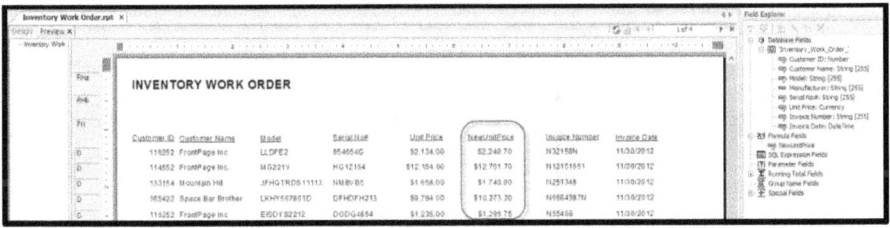

Figure 6.6 – Inventory Work Order has "New Unit Price."

Previously you have learned how to create a simple formula, and now let's find out more about what elements that builds formulas in Crystal Reports

Operator

Operators are symbols or words that perform the calculation inside a formula. There are twelve types of Operator in Crystal Reports. Here are some of the most common used.

Chapter 6 – FORMULAS and FUNCTIONS

1. Arithmetic

Arithmetic operators are: **Addition, Subtraction, Multiplication, Division, Percent, Integer Division, Modulus, Negative, and Exponentiation**, as shown below in figure 6.7.

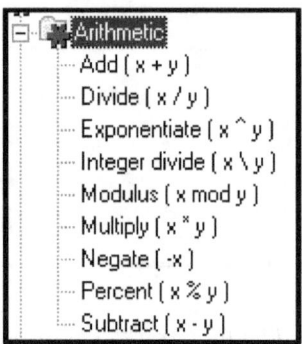

Figure 6.7 – Arithmetic Operators

When you use the Arithmetic operators, make sure to use parentheses to force the calculation to get calculation correctly. Some of the Arithmetic operators are applied in the basic formula previously.

2. Arrays

Arrays are the set of numbers or objects that follow a particular pattern. In Crystal Reports, Arrays a list of values that are of the same type. An Array in Crystal Reports only can be created using a square bracket (**[ ]**)

Chapter 6 – FORMULAS and FUNCTIONS

3. Boolean

Boolean generates conditions for control structures. In the order of precedence from the highest to lowest, these are Boolean operators; **Not**, **And**, **Or**, **Xor**, **Eqv**, and **Imp**.

4. Comparisons

The Comparison operator is to compare operands for a condition in control structure such as an IF expression. These are the example of Comparison operators; equal (=), not equal (<>), less than (<), greater than (>), less than or equal (<=) and greater or equal to (>=)

5. Control Structure

Control Structure operator is to expand the formula when it gets evaluated. It enables to vary the rigid sequence. Control Structure is branching within the formula.

For example:

If {table.column} = "Condition 1" then "result set1"
else If {table.column} = "Condition 2" then "result set2"
else If {table.column} = "Condition 3" then "result set3"
and so on.

Chapter 6 – FORMULAS and FUNCTIONS

6. Other

Another operator can be used like to comment out the formula. For example:

//{'Inventory_Work_Order_'.UnitPrice}+
({'Inventory_Work_Order_'.Unit Price} * 0.05)

Sample of formulas

- Extract **year** from *InvoiceDate*
  Year ({'Inventory_Work_Order_'.InvoiceDate})

- Age of **InvoiceDate** from **current date**
  Year (**CurrentDate**) - **Year** ({'Inventory_Work_Order_'.InvoiceDate})

- Display day from InvoiceDate
  Day ({'Inventory_Work_Order_'.Invoice Date})

- Extract **right 3 positions** from *Model*
  Right ({'Inventory_Work_Order_'.Model},3) **or**
  {'Inventory_Work_Order_'.Model} [1 to 3]

Chapter 6 – FORMULAS and FUNCTIONS

- Find the length of customer name:
  Len ({'Inventory_Work_Order_'.Customer Name})

- Change customer name to upper case:
  Uppercase ({'Inventory_Work_Order_'.Customer Name})

- Change customer name to lower case:
  Lowercase ({'Inventory_Work_Order_'.Customer Name})

- Convert **strings** to **numbers**:
  ToNumber ({'Inventory_Work_Order_'.Customer ID})

- Convert **numbers** to **strings**
  ToText (**ToNumber** ({'Inventory_Work_Order_'.Customer ID}))

- Round up:
  Round ({@NewUnitPrice})

Chapter 7– SUBREPORTS

What Is Subreports?

Subreports are designed the same like standard reports, but they embedded within the main report as report object. The purpose why we create Subreports is to have two independent, unrelated reports or different views in one single main report.

What is the difference between normal/standard report and Subreports? A normal/standard report will have Page Header while Subreports is a report(s) within the main report, therefore Subreports cannot have the Page Header at all.

Now, how do we add or insert Subreports into the standard main report? You will need to develop the standard main report and another report(s) but without the Page Header as none standard report(s). Then insert those Subreports into the main report on the Report Footer section to either unlinked or linked their parameter(s) to main report's parameter(s) so they can be related or linked to the main report.

In this chapter, I am using three reports called, **Labor Distribution (by work) Section.rdl**, **Home Labor Utilization Section.rdl** and **Job Distribution by Employee Section.rdl**.

Type of Subreports

There are two types of Subreports. Unlinked Subreports and linked Subreports.

Unlinked Subreports are a standalone report(s), and their data do not link each other with the main report. So with unlinked Subreports, the dataset can be different from different data source.

Chapter 7– SUBREPORTS

Linked Subreports where the dataset shares the same data source with the main report.

Insert Subreports

In this example, I am going to show you how to insert linked Subreports where later you will see how the dataset related to the main report and shared the same parameters values as well. Are you ready?

So, I made the **Labor Distribution (by work) Section.rdl** as the main report. The other two reports, **Home Labor Utilization Section.rdl** and **Job Distribution by Employee Section.rdl** are none Standard/normal report which what we called the Subreports. Both of these SubReports do not have the Page Header, as shown below in figure 7.0.a, 7.0.b, 7.0.c.

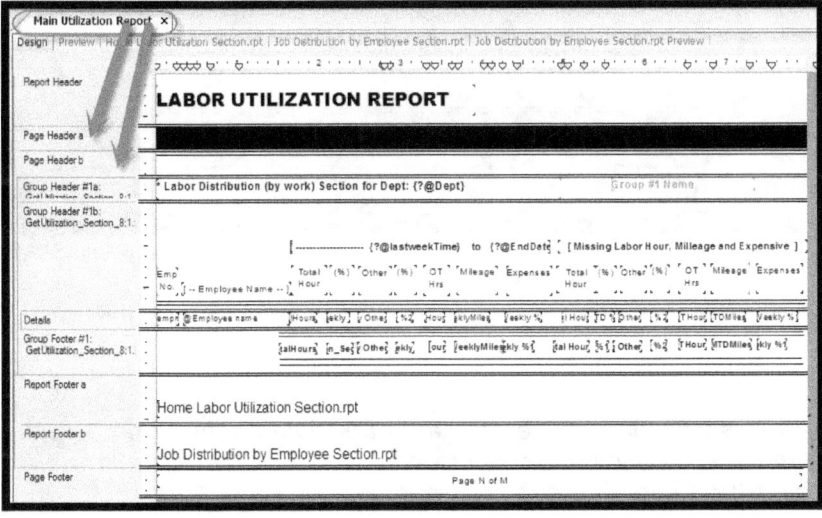

Figure 7.0.a – Labor Distribution (by work) Section.rdl as the main report with Page Header

Chapter 7 – SUBREPORTS

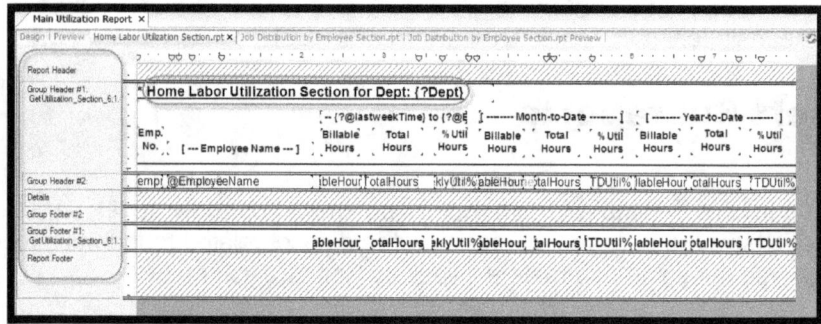

Figure 7.0.b – *Home Labor Utilization Section.rdl does not have the Page Header*

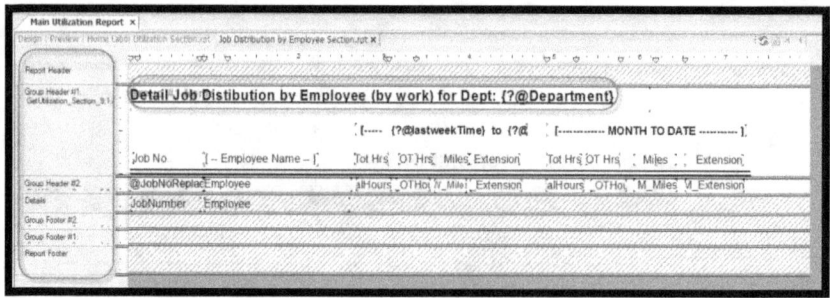

Figure 7.0.c – *Job Distribution by Employee Section.rdl does not have the Page Header*

Let's open our main report, **Labor Distribution (by work) Section.rdl**, and insert our first Subreports, **Home Labor Utilization Section.rdl** to Report Footer a, as shown below in figure 7.1.a.

Chapter 7– SUBREPORTS

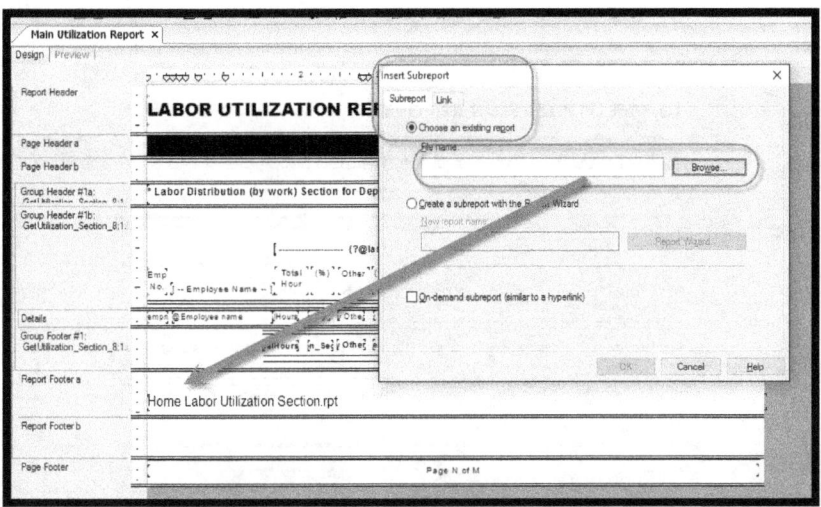

Figure 7.1.a – *Insert Home Labor Utilization Section.rdl to main report on the Report Footer section*

Repeat the above steps to insert second Subreports, **Job Distribution by Employee Section.rdl,** but place this report on Report Footer b, as shown below in figure 7.1.b.

Chapter 7– SUBREPORTS

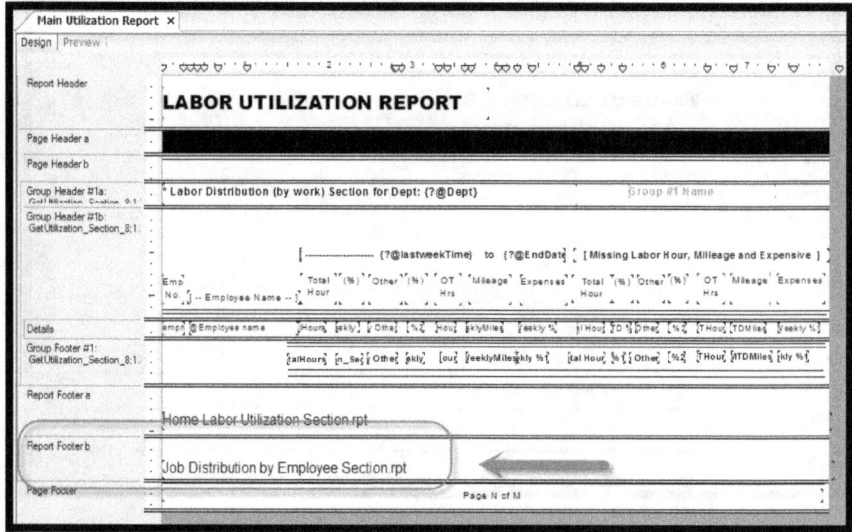

Figure 7.1.b – Insert **Job Distribution by Employee Section.rdl** to Report Footer b

Great! You just learned how to insert Subreports to the main report! Now let's link their parameters' values.

Link Subreports

Before we do that, let's take a look what parameters we have on each report.

Report name: **Labor Distribution (by work) Section.rdl** has four parameters;
1. @StartDateTime
2. @Lastweektime
3. @EndDatetime
4. @Dept.

Chapter 7– SUBREPORTS

Report name: ***Home Labor Utilization Section.rdl*** has four parameters;
1. *@StartDateTime*
2. *@Lastweektime*
3. *@EndDatetime*
4. *@Dept*

Report name: ***Job Distribution by Employee Section.rdl*** has four parameters;
1. *@StartDateTime*
2. *@Lastweektime*
3. *@EndDatetime*
4. *@Department.*

As you can see on the above, each report shared the same parameters type. So what you need to do is to link each of the parameter from two Subreports' reports to the main report.

On the main report of the Design tab on the top menu bar, Select "**Edit**" and choose "**Subreports Links**", as shown below in figure 7.2.

Chapter 7 – SUBREPORTS

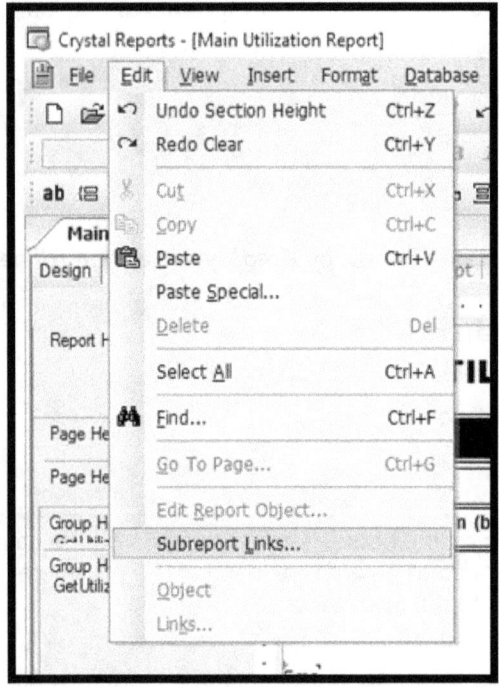

Figure 7.2 – *Select "Subreports links" to link parameters values to main report*

On the Subreports links window, select one of the Subreports to link to the main report. In this example, I am going to select **Home Labor Utilization Section.rdl**, as shown below in figure 7.3.

Chapter 7– SUBREPORTS

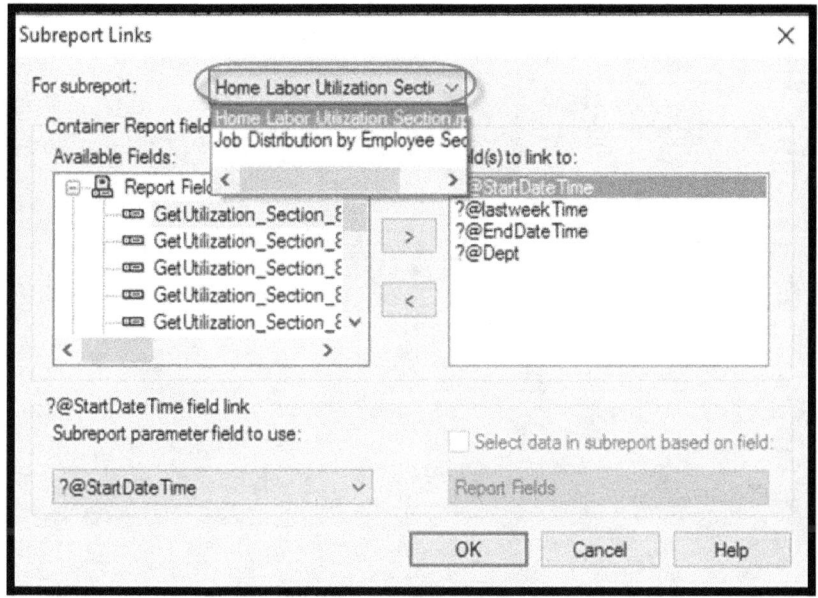

Figure 7.3 – Home Labor Utilization Section.rdl for Subreports

Once you selected the **Home Labor Utilization Section.rdl**, on the "**Available Fields**", scroll down until you see all the parameter(s) on this report then use the "**>**" button to move each one of them to the "**Field(s) to link to:**" area, as shown below in figure 7.4.

Note: The "*Field(s) to link to"* is the area that lists all the main report's parameter(s) is.

Chapter 7– SUBREPORTS

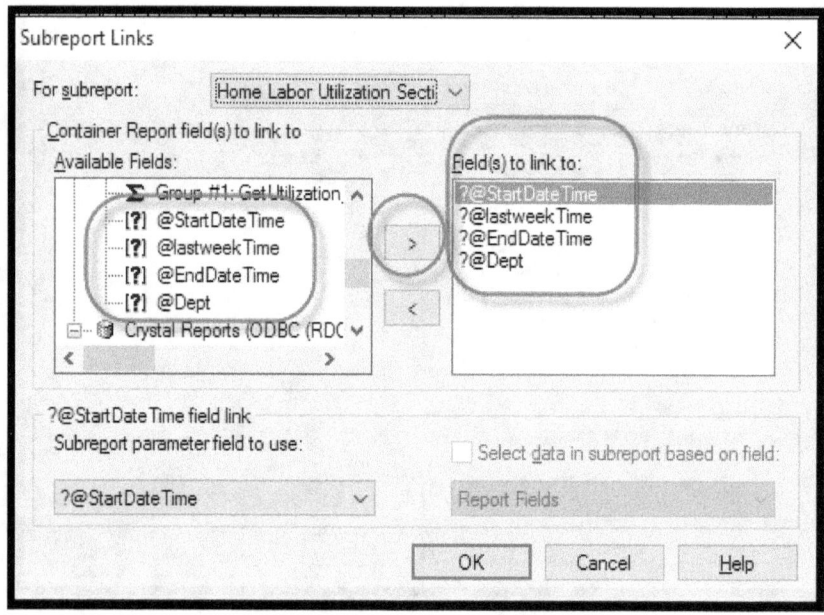

Figure 7.4 – Move each parameter to "Field(s) to link to" area

Now, start from the first parameter of the **Home Labor Utilization Section.rdl**, highlight the **@StartDateTime** from the "**Fields(s) to link to:**" then on the "**Subreport parameter field to use:**" select the **@StartDateTime** then click **OK** (where we link the **@StartDateTime** parameter of the main report's parameter, as shown below in figure 7.5.a

Chapter 7– SUBREPORTS

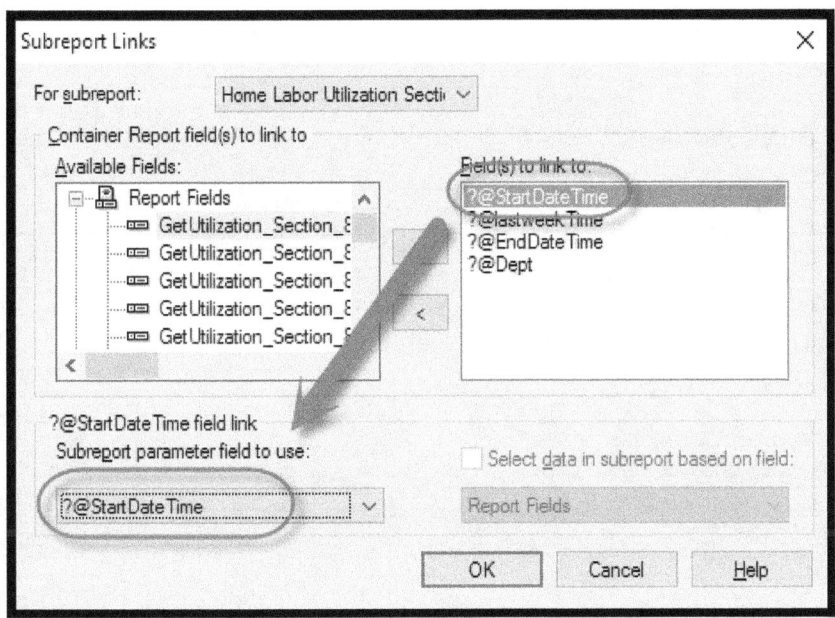

Figure 7.5.a – Link @StartDateTime from Subreports to the main report

Congratulations, you have learned how to link a parameter from Subreports to the main report. This is a great job!!!

Now let's continue to link the second parameter of *@LastWeekTime*. Of the Subreports links window, highlight our second parameter of *@LastWeekTime* of the "***Field(s) to link to:***" and "***Subreport Parameter field to use:***" as shown below in figure 7.5.b

Chapter 7– SUBREPORTS

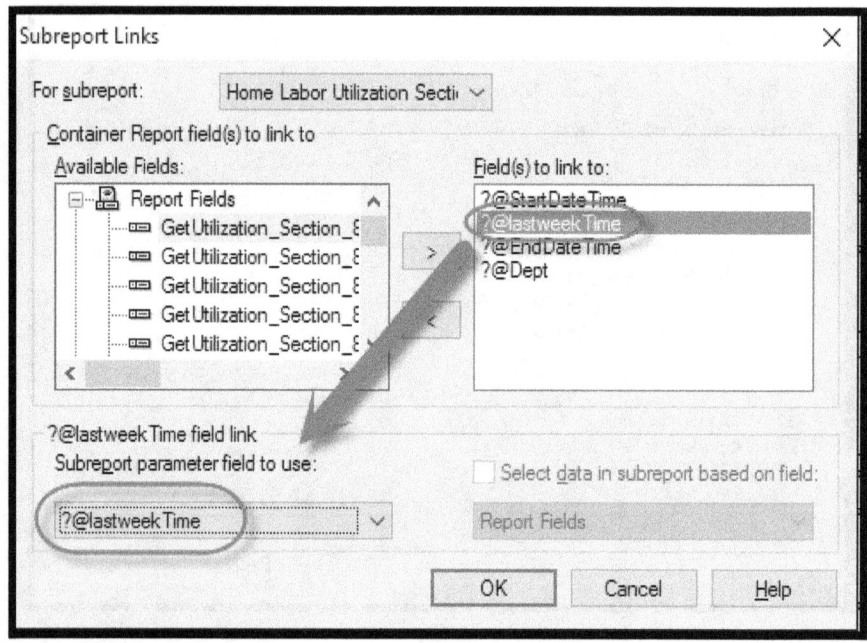

Figure 7.5.b – *Link @LastWeekTime from Subreports to the main report.*

Repeat the process like what we just did on:

@StartDateTime, @LastWeekTime, @EndDateTime and *@Dept*. Click **OK** to complete this process, as shown below in figure 7.5.c. and 7.5.d.

Chapter 7 – SUBREPORTS

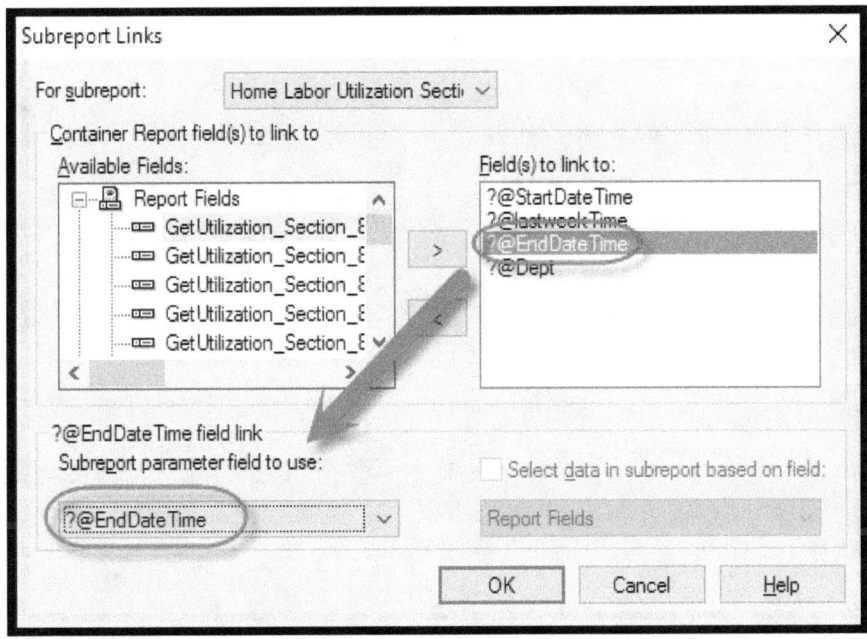

Figure 7.5.c *– Link @EndDateTime from Subreports to the main report*

Chapter 7– SUBREPORTS

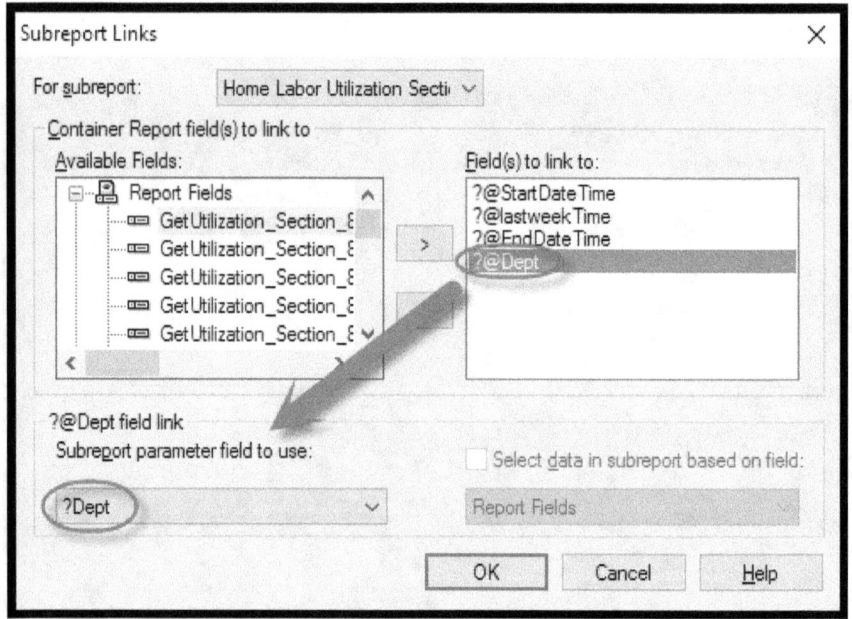

Figure 7.5.d – *Link @Dept from Subreports to main report*

Great! We just linked all the parameters from our **Home Labor Utilization Section.rdl** Subreports to **Labor Distribution (by work) Section.rdl**.

Let's do the same process to our second Subreports, *Job Distribution by Employee Section.rdl.*

From the "**Subreport Link**" window, now select our second subreports, *Job Distribution by Employee Section.rdl*, as shown below in figure 7.6.a.

Chapter 7– SUBREPORTS

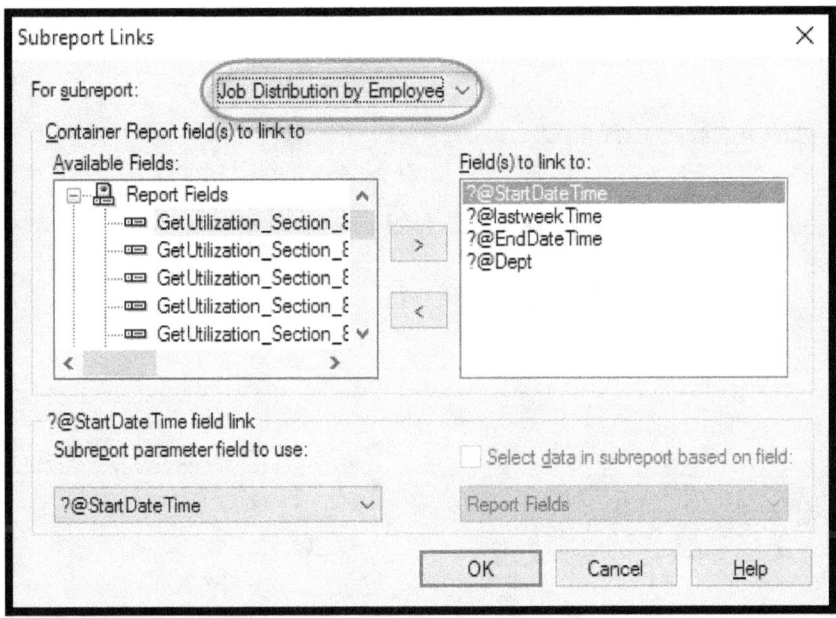

Figure 7.6.a – Select the second Subreports, Job Distribution by Employee Section.rdl

Now, let's link our second Subreports' parameters to the main report. Do the same process steps we did earlier with our first Subreports, **Home Labor Utilization Section.rdl.**

Let's link the @StartDateTime, as shown below in figure 7.6.b.

Chapter 7– SUBREPORTS

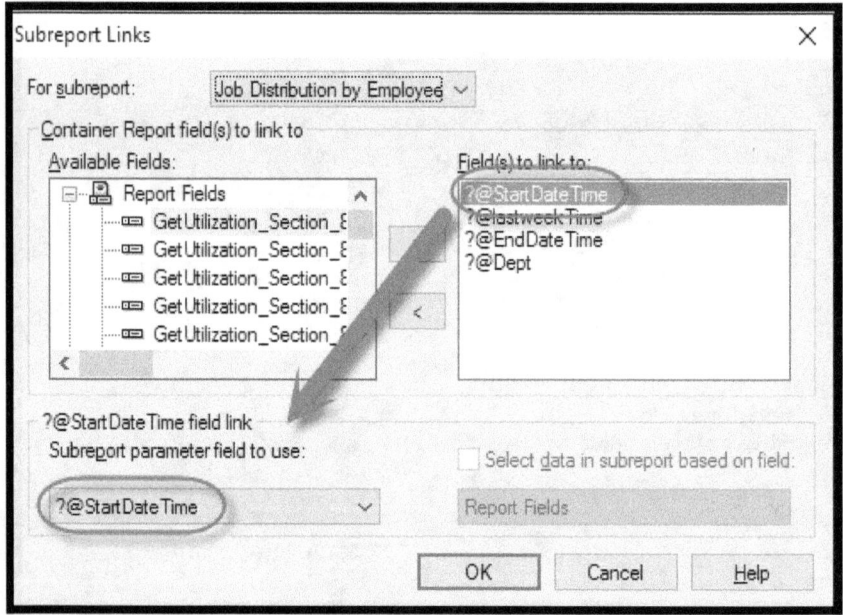

Figure 7.6.b – *Link the @StartDateTime parameter from the second Subreports, Job Distribution by Employee Section.rdl to the main report.*

Repeat the same steps for @LastWeekTime, @sEndDateTime and @Dept then click **OK** to complete this process, as shown below in figure 7.6.c, 7.6.d and 7.6.e.

Chapter 7– SUBREPORTS

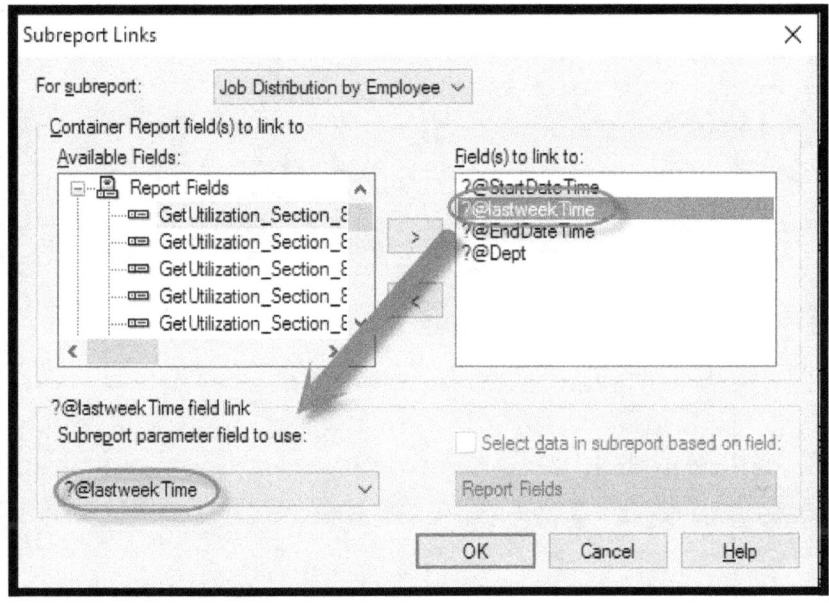

Figure 7.6.c – Link @LastWeekTime from Subreports to the main report

Chapter 7– SUBREPORTS

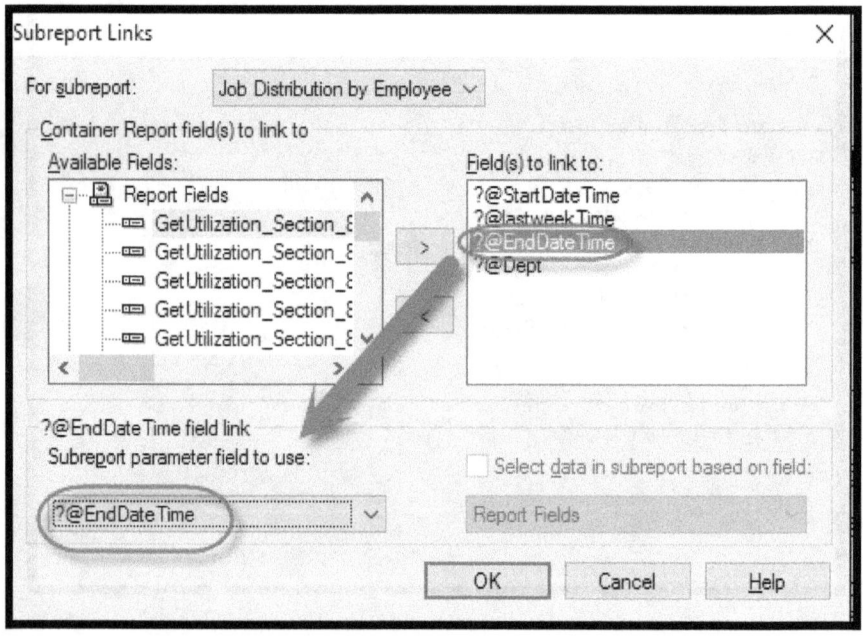

Figure 7.6.d – *Link @EndDateTime from Subreports to the main report*

Chapter 7– SUBREPORTS

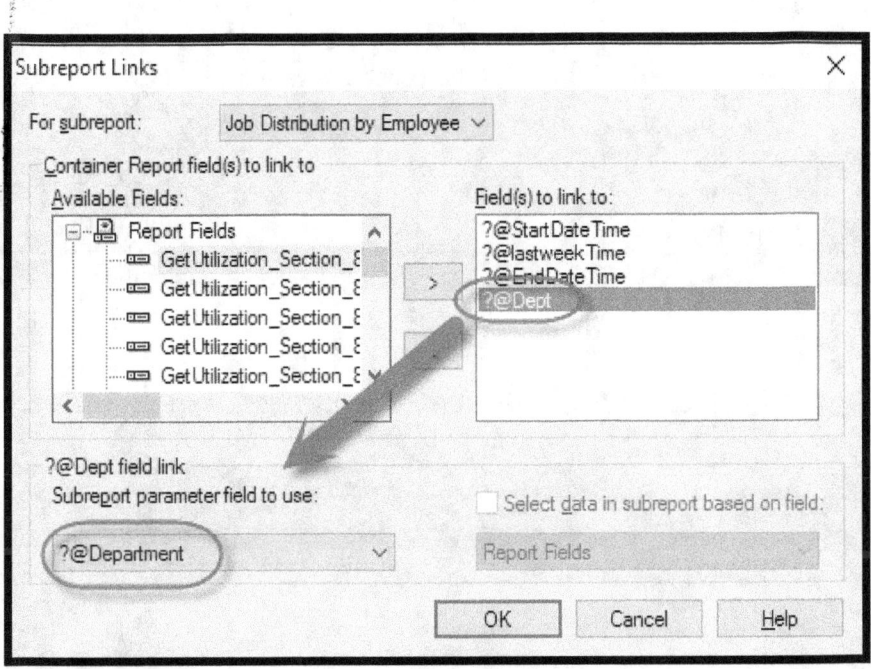

Figure 7.6.e – Link @Department from Subreports to @Dept of the main report

Congratulations!!! You have learned how to insert and link the parameters between the main report and Subreports.

Reporting with
VISUAL
CRYSTAL REPORTS

Helmy Alexcia

www.ingramcontent.com/pod-product-compliance
Lightning Source LLC
Chambersburg PA
CBHW060836170526
45158CB00001B/176